THE SONG OF SONGS

Textual Commentary and Theological Reflections

The Song of Songs

TEXTUAL COMMENTARY AND THEOLOGICAL REFLECTIONS

Lawrence R. Farley

ST VLADIMIR'S SEMINARY PRESS
YONKERS, NEW YORK
2018

Library of Congress Cataloging-in-Publication Data

Names: Farley, Lawrence R., author.

Title: The Song of songs : textual commentary and theological reflections / Lawrence R. Farley.

Description: Yonkers, NY : St Vladimir's Seminary Press, 2018. | Includes bibliographical references.

Identifiers: LCCN 2017057732 (print) | LCCN 2017058746 (ebook) | ISBN 9780881416213 | ISBN 9780881416206 (alk. paper)

Subjects: LCSH: Bible. Song of Solomon—Commentaries.

Classification: LCC BS1485.53 (ebook) | LCC BS1485.53 .F375 2018 (print) | DCC 223/.9077—dc23

LC record available at https://lccn.loc.gov/ 2017057732

COPYRIGHT © 2018 BY
ST VLADIMIR'S SEMINARY PRESS
575 Scarsdale Road, Yonkers, NY 10707
1-800-204-2665
www.svspress.com

ISBN 978–0–88141–620–6 (print)
ISBN 978–0–88141–621–3 (electronic)

Dedicated to all Christian singles

who preserve their chastity

out of love for their heavenly bridegroom.

Contents

Time for a Song

Though every truth in Holy Scripture is timely, certain times cry out for particular truths more than others. Our own time is characterized by confusion about gender—both gender roles and the very nature of gender itself. Just as the fourth-century Church was characterized by controversy about the Person of Christ, our own day is troubled by controversy about personhood itself.

The confusion began with what was once quaintly called "Women's Lib," a movement that recognized real social inequities regarding the roles of women, and proffered a cure for those ills that turned out to be as bad or worse than the ills themselves. That is, the new movement not only offered political solutions to real and perceived problems, but also grounded those solutions in a philosophical reworking of the traditional relationship between man and woman, husband and wife, so as to pit the two genders against one another in adversarial roles. The new movement disdained woman's traditional roles as architect and ruler of home life (an action described in 1 Tim 5.14 as οἰκοδεσποτέω, *oikodespoteō*, "to manage one's household"[1]) and teacher of the children, deeming these roles too limiting and demeaning. Women were encouraged instead to have careers outside the home, even to become CEOs, because they needed to be liberated from the traditional role of housewife and mother, and from the cycle of sex leading to children and a life at home. Birth control and abortion were considered the indispensable tools needed to

---

[1] The function is one of authority. The cognate noun οἰκοδεσπότης (*oikodespotēs*) is translated by the NASB as "head of the house" in Mt 24.43, and as "master of the house" in the Arndt-Gingrich Lexicon.

strike off their shackles, and thus reproductive rights became a sacred cow within the feminist movement, the very bedrock upon which the movement was based.

The war on tradition quickly escalated, with sexuality the next domino to fall in a long line of traditional dominos. The language of civil rights, which had proved so effective in overturning the traditional understanding of a woman's role in the home, was taken up again to overturn the traditional understanding of sexuality as binary, involving a man and a woman. Some in the movement declared homosexual activity to be every bit as moral and valid as traditional heterosexuality, and very quickly the entire draconian apparatus of media and legislation was geared up to enforce conformity to the newly defined norms. Having liberated woman from her role as support for her husband and mother to the couple's children, feminists now sought to liberate the family from binary sexuality itself. Not only was the husband-wife relationship reconfigured, but now it is also in the process of being totally destroyed as normative. Other options present themselves: a woman might become the wife/ husband of another woman (some terminological shifts, of course, being necessary), just as a man might become the wife/husband of another man.

This would not be the last domino to fall, however, for the concept of "transgenderism" has now become the latest cause célèbre of the ideological left. This term refers not simply to cases of physical hermaphroditism (where both sets of genital organs are at least vestigially present), or to cases where doctors can detect the presence of unusually high levels of the hormones usually found in the opposite gender. The term now also refers to persons who simply declare themselves to be the opposite gender, even in the complete physical absence of any evidence to substantiate the declaration. If I feel like a woman and declare myself to be female, then I am a woman, on the basis of my subjective declaration alone. This position sunders subjective feeling from observable biology altogether, and in fact from any measurable reality for that matter. Transgender claims and demands have taken their place alongside other unassailable "human rights." No less a public personage than J. K. Rowling, with her considerable influence on youth, classes it along with women's suffrage as a basic civil right, thereby also declaring that anyone who protests the enforcement of transgender demands must be a throwback akin to those who denied that women should be allowed to vote.

The next domino to fall is anyone's guess (polygamy? polyamory?), but what is certain is that the transgender domino will not be the last to fall. A wash of sexual confusion, a pandemic of pornography, and a plague of rape and sexual violence has descended upon us like the judgment of God (which in fact it is), and we have barely begun to experience the terrible and terrifying fruits of these revolutionary changes. We have little understanding of the significance of either sex or virginity, or of the nature of love and its roots in the divine. Our children and grandchildren are growing up in a dangerous time.

What does all this mean? It means it is time for a song—in particular, it is time for Solomon's Song of Songs, for the song which emphatically asserts that human sexuality is binary, a joy shared between a man and a woman. This ancient collection of erotic love poetry, canonized as Scripture by both synagogue and Church, contains truths we need to hear now more than ever, especially truths about gender. This biblical book was never simply a collection of erotic love poetry, but always much, much more. The Jewish sages and Church Fathers long recognized this. The latter often grouped it with the two other biblical books traditionally ascribed to Solomon (Proverbs and Ecclesiastes, or Koheleth), placing it first as the summit of wisdom. They conceived the path to wisdom as threefold, consisting of purification, illumination, and union. One needed first to purge oneself from the grosser sins and then have one's inner eye illumined to see God's glory in the world, in order to finally achieve union with the divine. These three stages were the respective subjects, they said, of Proverbs (which offers the way of purification from folly and sin), Ecclesiastes (which teaches how to see wisdom in the ways of the world), and finally the Song of Songs as an allegory of the delight of the soul in its final union with the divine.

A Word About the Use of Allegory

St Gregory of Nyssa, standing within a venerable tradition of allegorical interpretation, produced a notable commentary on the Song of Songs, although his method now stands at odds with contemporary scholarship. The present volume seeks to follow in the footsteps of St Gregory and his fellow patristic writers, even if necessarily trailing some distance behind the genius of the great saints. That is, we will examine the Song of Songs not only for its historical meaning as a collection of love poems, but also mine it for its deep theological insights, making occasional reference to the commentary of the great bishop of Nyssa and others who wrote in that same tradition. Our own allegorical interpretations will be offered in a series of reflections embedded within an interpretive historical commentary, as excursuses within the total volume.[2] Throughout this volume, in other words, we will first offer a commentary on the historical meaning of the text, followed by a series of comments based on an allegorical reading of that same text. In this way the total interpretation of the Song will run on two parallel tracks, one historical and the other allegorical. We will offer a textual commentary and also theological comments. But before we begin, I would like to offer a word of justification for use of the allegorical method.

The allegorical approach to Scripture that was so highly valued by ancient writers, both Jewish and Christian, has fallen out of favor today, and it is not difficult to see why. Any text is susceptible to a number of allegorical interpretations, each one seemingly arbitrary and subject to no discernable control. Thus, for example, the Jewish scholar Rashi allegorizes Song 1.13 ("My beloved is to me a pouch of

---

[2]The translation of the text is my own. The text will be distinguished from the commentary through the use of a different font. When the text is cited in the commentary, it will be in italics.

myrrh, which lies all night between my breasts") as referring to the Shekinah presence of God that rested between the two cherubim above the ark of the covenant; St Cyril of Alexandria, on the other hand, allegorizes the verse as referring to Christ standing between the two covenants, Old and New.[3] With such apparently endless interpretive possibilities at hand, surely the most sensible course would seem to be to avoid allegory completely, accepting only the historical and literal meaning of the text. How else might the interpreter avoid the pitfalls—and sometimes even complete absurdities—of arbitrary allegorization?

An Orthodox interpreter will not so easily abandon a method that won the assent of so many Church Fathers. Nonetheless, the allegorical approach to finding deeper meaning must be pursued carefully. In particular, the allegorical and deeper meaning must always be located along a specific theological trajectory, for only then can the dangers of arbitrary allegorization be avoided. In the Song of Songs, that trajectory is provided by an examination of the deeper meaning of human love.

When we look at human love, we find that it has its ultimate source in God. Man is made in God's image, and part of this divine image in man consists in our capacity for self-transcendence and self-sacrifice, in our ability to find our own meaning in the other person, even to lay down our life for that other person—in other words, in love. Our relationship with the "thou" whom we behold is crucial for our becoming an authentic "I," for just as being is rooted in communion, authentic human personhood is rooted in love. And since God is the original and we are but his derivative image, his divine love is the original and our human love derives from it. Human love has divine love as its ultimate source.

Because human love is rooted in the divine love, marriage—the most fruitful expression of love between two persons—is an image of the love of God for humanity. God loves us and gives himself

[3] J. Cheryl Exum, *Song of Songs: A Commentary* (Louisville, KY: Westminster John Knox Press, 2005), 76.

totally and unreservedly (the depth of which we glimpse in the incarnation), just as a bridegroom gives himself to his bride. God is the bridegroom; humanity—the individual soul—is the bride. God is the lover, we are his beloved. He is the seeker; we are the sought. He is active; we are responsive. He is (typologically) the male, and all created souls are feminine to him. When transposed into historical and covenantal terms, Yahweh is the bridegroom and Israel is his bride. And in the new covenant Christ is the bridegroom and the Church the bride, as Paul famously teaches (Eph 5.31–32). Thus, God's love for mankind is the model and prototype, with marriage its human expression and mirror. God's perfect and non-sexual love for humanity finds a faint, imperfect, and partial mirror in the sexual love between man and woman, husband and wife.

This means that when we read the Song of Songs as a celebration of the divine love between God and man, we are not misreading the text but rather exploring its authentic deeper meaning. The text concerns not only the sexual relationship between man and woman, but also the relationship between Christ and his Church, for it is about love, both human and divine. We see this love primarily through the sexual relationship between husband and wife, but at the same time these human dynamics also conceal insights regarding the divine relationship between Christ and us.

This connection between human sexuality, i.e., marriage, and God's love for his people is not arbitrary, and thus the exegetical tradition that reads the Song as yielding insights into the Church's union with Christ should not be disdained, however much it has fallen from modern scholarly favor.[4] When Paul interprets the sexual material in the Genesis creation story as containing "a great

---

[4]One example of such modern rejection of allegory is Duane Garrett, who in *Song of Songs*, Word Biblical Commentary, vol. 23B (Nashville, TN: Thomas Nelson Publishers, 2004) wrote, "To read a single allegorical interpretation is to be impressed, and to wonder if the author is onto something profound; to read a hundred allegorical interpretations is to be depressed, and to want to discard the whole. . . . I do not believe that the allegorization of any text of the Song is of theological or exegetical value" (74, 76).

mystery" and as "speaking of Christ and the Church" (Eph 5.32), he is not indulging in an arbitrary or fanciful reading of the text. The Old Testament is replete with sexual imagery used to describe the union of God and his people.

Take, for example, Ezekiel 16.8. Here the prophet Ezekiel, in an extended allegory, portrays Israel in terms of a young abandoned girl rescued by God and cared for by him until she reached puberty and "the time for love." God then declares that he will "spread his skirt over her" to take her in marriage (cf. Ruth 3.9), only to discover later that she rejects his love for the sake of other lovers. Or look at Isa 62.4–5, in which God says to Jerusalem, "You will be called 'My delight is in her,' and your land, 'Married,' for as a young man marries a virgin, so your sons will marry you; and as the bridegroom rejoices over the bride, so your God will rejoice over you." Indeed, a favorite term for Jerusalem is "the virgin daughter of Zion" (Is 37.22; Jer 14.17; Lam 2.13; Zeph 3.14; Zech 2.10). Another example can be found in Jer 3.1–8, in which God speaks of Israel as his unfaithful wife who leaves him for another man (3.1) and is given a certificate of divorce (3.8). Or consider the life and words of the prophet Hosea, whom God instructs to use his personal marital tragedy as an image of God's own heartbreak (Hos 2.2–20). God speaks to Hosea about Israel as his own wife—a wife that abandoned him for other lovers.

We see here a long and consistent tradition portraying the relationship between God and his people as the relationship between husband and wife. These texts represent metaphors, not strict allegories, but the comparison between the marriage covenant and the divine covenant is clear nonetheless. When St Paul interprets marriage between man and woman in Genesis as foreshadowing the relationship between Christ and his Church, he is simply continuing along a well-worn path. God is the lover and redeemed creation his beloved. In this sense all souls are feminine to him. That is why the Church must be a bride, not a bridegroom—a mother Church, not a father Church.

This tradition provides the foundation for our allegorical approach to reading the Song. It does not, however, posit a one-to-one correspondence between the sexual imagery offered in the text and a spiritual reality. Such a one-to-one correspondence of symbol to the thing symbolized does indeed run the risk of arbitrary attribution, which some might consider to have been the case with Rashi and St Cyril of Alexandria. Such examples have led virtually every modern commentator to disallow allegorical interpretation altogether. The Song, however, is not an allegory in the same sense that *Pilgrim's Progress* is an allegory, with each item or name in the text symbolizing something else. Such an understanding only leads us to exegetical dead ends, for we can never know for certain which spiritual reality is symbolized by any given sexual image. Rather, we suggest that understanding the plain meaning of the text allows us to gain further insight into our relationship with God, since sexual love is an echo and image of the divine love that Christ has for his Church.

This approach to allegory is not identical to that of St Gregory of Nyssa, nor to the Alexandrian tradition in which he stood. Because that tradition tended to minimize the sanctity of sexuality, it did not perceive a direct trajectory from sexual love to divine love. The Alexandrian tradition posited an inner discontinuity between the symbol and the thing symbolized, with the inevitable result that some symbols appear arbitrary. For St Gregory, sexual passion and its imagery provide only a distant pointer to spiritual realities. The sexual symbol might direct the reader across an abyss to a distant and dissimilar spiritual reality, but it could not partake of the reality itself. Thus St Gregory, in his prefatory letter to Olympias about his homilies on the Song of Songs, speaks of the text being "cleansed [*kekatharmenēn*] of its obvious literal sense by undefiled thoughts," for the latter alone allowed "the philosophy hidden in the words" to be "brought to light."[5]

[5]Gregory of Nyssa, *Homilies on the Song of Songs*, Preface (*Gregorii Nysseni Opera*, vol. 6, p. 4). Translation in *Gregory of Nyssa: Homilies on the Song of Songs*,

In contrast to this approach, we will seek the primary layer of meaning in the plain wording of the text itself, confident that the God who created them male and female (Gen 1.27) will provide significant insights even in the "obvious literal sense." (In this sense our approach will conform more closely to that of St John Chrysostom and the Antiochian tradition, which while not rejecting allegory sought to ground the meaning in the literal text.) The text does not require cleansing, but mining. With all respect to the great Nicene saint of Nyssa, his appreciation for Origen and for the Platonic tradition in which they both were formed did not serve him well when it came to finding spiritual meaning in the letter of this particular text. His protestation to the contrary notwithstanding,[6] sometimes the letter can also give life. The letter, or obvious literal sense of the Scripture, is "profitable for training in righteousness" as it stands (2 Tim 3.16), and does not require help from allegory to become profitable. However, the allegorical interpretation, when grounded in the literal, may yield further insights for those who would continue digging into the text. We believe that the literal meaning can and does provide true symbols for the thing symbolized, because sexual love is true love and therefore partakes, however partially, of the divine love. The allegorical meaning of the text is the result of finding the literal and sexual meaning of the text, and transposing it into the deeper setting of divine love. If one defines "allegory" as a strict one-to-one correspondence between a symbol and the thing symbolized—a set of correspondences, a string of metaphors that allow the narrative to be read on a higher level—then perhaps our present method might more appropriately be called transposition rather than allegory.

Richard A. Norris Jr., trans. and ed. (Atlanta, GA: Society of Biblical Literature, 2012), 3.

[6]Thus in his letter to Olympias cited above, Gregory writes, "This . . . is why [Paul] says 'The letter kills but the spirit gives life' (2 Cor 3:6), for frequently the narrative, if we stop short at the mere events, does not furnish us with models of the good life. How does it profit the cause of a virtuous life to hear . . . that Isaiah went in to the prophetess (Isa 8:3), if one stops short at the literal sense?" Ibid (*GNO* 6:7). Translation in *Homilies*, 5, 7.

A Brief Word About the Song as Dramatic Narrative

Some interpretations read the Song as a dramatic narrative containing not two but three characters: King Solomon, the girl, and a third character, a humble shepherd boy who is the girl's true love. In some versions of this interpretation, the girl finds herself courted by King Solomon to become part of his harem, but she rejects his royal advances and remains true to her first love. The advantage of this reading of the Song is that one can read literally the references to the man as king (for example, in 1.4) and also as shepherd (see 1.7), thus making a firm distinction between the exalted but formal Solomon in 3.6f and 8.12 and the beloved, familiar shepherd lover in 1.7 and 6.2. But there remain problems with this reading of the text.

First, such a dramatic reading makes any consistent application of allegory difficult. If the shepherd is an image of Christ, the soul's true love, then who does his wicked rival Solomon represent? Furthermore, the woman's references to the king—who remains unnamed but is clearly Solomon, given the Song's superscription— are full of love. They do not read like a rejection of the king in favor of someone else, e.g., 1.2–4, 1.12–13. It seems odd for the woman to say longingly, "Let him kiss me with the kisses of his mouth" (1.2) if we are to understand her next line ("The king has brought me into his chambers") as a cry of distress at being brought into those chambers. The words read most naturally if the entry into the king's chambers fulfills her desire for his kisses.

Or consider 1.12, where the woman declares that while the king was on his couch her *nard* (or desire) gave forth its fragrance, and she describes her beloved as a *pouch of myrrh* lying between her breasts. It seems odd that the sight of the king lying on his couch would lead the woman to describe with longing her passion for someone else. Once again, the text reads most naturally if the love the woman describes while she is with the king is her love for the king.

In summary, we can understand the Song as a three-person drama only by continually reading into the text an arbitrary, preconceived plot line with little apparent connection to the actual words of the text. The text is difficult enough to understand without such further complications. For this reason the natural reading is to be preferred, wherein there are two voices, those of the man and the woman, with an occasional chorus. The praises of the woman for the man and of the man for the woman are best read as the lovers' mutual praise and delight in each other.

A Word About Authorship and Structure

Finally, let us offer a few comments about the Song's authorship and outline. Contemporary scholarship today all but universally denies Solomonic authorship,[7] though this is more often asserted than actually proven.[8] Given the ascription to Solomon in 1.1, as well as the references to Solomon in 3.7, 3.9, 3.11, 8.11, and other repeated references to the male lover as a king, I would suggest that in the absence of compelling reasons to the contrary we must accept that it was either authored by Solomon or written about him under royal sponsorship. Commentators often cite the reference in 1 Kings 4.32 to his authorship of a thousand and five songs as the inspiration for a later attribution of the Song to him. However, if he did indeed write (or collect) a thousand and five songs, there is no reason why our present Song could not have been among them. It seems perverse to read the historical evidence for Solomon's wide learning and vast literary output to support the idea that he did not, in fact, write what our text says that he did. It may be true that the words of the superscription in 1.1 ("The song of songs which is Solomon's")[9] come from a hand other than the one that wrote the Song itself,[9] but this in itself does nothing to disprove Solomonic authorship of the text that

[7]A modern scholar who accepts a Solomonic provenance or authorship is Garrett, *Song of Songs*, 22f.

[8]John G. Snaith, for example, simply writes, "Solomonic authorship is probably a literary fiction, as in Proverbs and the Wisdom of Solomon," without adducing any further argument. See his *Song of Songs*, New Century Bible Commentary (Grand Rapids, MI: Wm. B. Eerdmans Publishing Company, 1993), 8.

[9]For example Snaith, *The Song of Songs*, 13.

follows. When we find the *lamed auctoris*, i.e., the *lamed* of author-ship,[10] in the Psalter, e.g., Psalm 56.1, which describes this psalm as *le-David*, it is interpreted as meaning that the psalm in question was written by David, or at least concerns him. There is no compelling reason to deny the *lamed* of *le-Shlomo* the same force here, even if we were to interpret the *lamed* in the sense of "owned by Solomon" (cf. 1 Kg 10.28, which uses wording identical to Song 1.1, the so-called "*lamed* of possession").

But ascribing to the text Solomonic authorship or provenance does not require us to interpret it as Solomonic autobiography, nor to determine exactly who his beloved might be (for example, Pharaoh's daughter; cf. 1 Kg 3.1). The Song is more poetic than autobiographical, for the male lover in the text declares his love in emphatically exclusive terms, while the historical Solomon had little commitment to such monogamy (1 Kg 11.3). Although Solomon or another unnamed king features prominently as the male lover throughout the text (1.4, 1.5, 1.12, 3.7, 3.9, 3.11, 7.5), Solomon is not featured either personally or by name as one of the *dramatis personae*. He never announces himself to his beloved or says, "I, King Solomon, love you!" The text conceals personal identity, subordinat-ing it to the over-arching purpose of celebrating the mutual delight between man and woman. As our textual commentary will make clear, King Solomon is presented as the male lead because a king was considered the epitome of desirability, wealth, elegance, and fame. However, the man in the Song represents not King Solomon as an individual, but every male lover. Likewise, the woman in the Song represents not one particular person in King Solomon's life, but every female lover.

The Song is therefore a celebration of human sexuality and lovers' delight rather than a window into King Solomon's personal life. Recognizing this frees us from the need to force the details of

---

[10]*Lamed* is the twelfth letter of the Hebrew alphebet. When used as a prefix, it can mean "by," "of," "to," or "for" (the first of these possible uses, when prefixed to an author's name, is the "*lamed* of authorship").—*Ed.*

the Song into a precise historical setting, such as trying to reconcile how a king could call on his beloved at her home without his retinue, or find time to pasture his own flocks. These details belong to the poetry and contribute to the creation of an idyllic, pastoral world of love. The lover is both king and shepherd; the lovers meet in his royal chamber, in the woods, at her home, and in the streets of the city. The images are separate and varied ingredients in a long poem that surveys in detail the many moods and places of love, rather than consistent parts of a single coherent narrative.

Neither do I regard the Song as an anthology of separate songs, each written by a different author. The Song's consistent use of imagery and voice throughout witnesses to a single author, e.g., the repetition of the adjuration in 2.7, 3.5, and 5.8. Affirming a single author, however, does not involve asserting that the author has written a narrative. It seems that we have in the Song a series of individual images, fantasies, reminiscences, daydreams, each celebrating the mutual love between the man and the woman. Producing a convincing plot outline of the Song is difficult (as witnessed by the many different outlines already suggested by scholars), and furthermore such plots require a good deal of reading the plot into the text itself. There seems to be no connecting thread that joins these separate poetic celebrations, and therefore no clear narrative undergirding the poems. Solomon's marriage is mentioned in 3.6–11, but it seems the couple were intimate before that point (cf. references to their "couch," 1.16; their passionate embrace, 2.6; and her bringing him to the room in which she was conceived, 3.4). Nor are there any firm links between the various lovers' dialogues that enable us to place them within a continuing narrative. It seems as if the Song offers us the opportunity to overhear the lovers in their ongoing romance, in varied circumstances. What matters is not narrative plot, but the beauty of their romance and their love.

Outline of the Song of Songs

1. 1.1: Superscription: The Song of Songs, which is Solomon's
2. 1.2–4: The Woman longs for the King's love
3. 1.5–2.7: The Woman seeks the King among his flock
4. 2.8–17: The Man comes to the home of his beloved
5. 3.1–5: The Woman seeks her lover by night
6. 3.6–11: The marriage of King Solomon
7. 4.1–5.1: The Man woos his beloved
8. 5.2–6.3: The Woman rejects her lover and then seeks him
9. 6.4–13: The Man praises his beloved's face
10. 7.1–8.4: The Man and the Woman spend the night in the open field
11. 8.5–7: The Man and the Woman return together from the wilderness
12. 8.8–12: The Woman's independence
13. 8.13–14: The Man and the Woman's final exchange

We note throughout the Song the theme of the joy of sexual union between man and woman. Marriage is an assumed societal reality and considered good (3.11, 8.6), but it forms no part of the narrative, nor even of the poetry. Indeed, in one part of the Song (3.1–5) the woman, missing her lover night after night, leaves her bed to seek him in the streets of the city and take him back home with her. If they were married, why would she not simply have waited until his return to their marriage bed the next day? We misread the Song, however, if we conclude that it is somehow celebrating what was once called "free love," or justifying extramarital sex. Such celebration was hardly the case in ancient Israel. The Song is poetry, not ethics; it celebrates the glory of love's desire without addressing the question of how such desire may be ethically satisfied. The Song presents the secret trysts as part of the deliciousness of secret love, as one part of love's varied delights. The author took for granted that such sweetness can only be tasted within marriage. The Song offers us an almost delirious reveling in the desires to be found between a man and a woman, not a manual for righteous living. The Song celebrates the glory of romantic love *in itself,* without denying that socially it is enjoyed within marriage.

More importantly, in our present time of demonic noise, the Song offers us a divine melody for the heart. In a time of gender confusion, it offers us reaffirmation; in a time of pornography-inspired depression, it offers us a joy that descends from heaven to earth, a gift from God to cheer, inspire, and guide. The Song represents an opening to the paradise of love between the first man and his bride, a garden from which our race has long been banished. A rabbi once said[11] that all of eternity in its entirety was not as worthy as the day on which this Song was given to Israel. Let us begin by listening to the first notes of that heavenly and paradisal song.

[11] Rabbi Akiba, in the early second century.

1

Superscription: The Song of Songs, which is Solomon's

The term "song of songs" does not indicate that the text consists of a collection of different songs, but rather that this Song is a superlative one, of superior quality, the best of songs, just as the term "the holy of holies" means "the holiest place of all." The title thus offers us not just any song but a transcendent and glorious theme, one fit for Solomon himself.

If Solomon was not the actual author of the Song,[1] then its attribution to him ("which is Solomon's") becomes all the more significant. In Ecclesiastes 1.1, the figure of "the son of David, king in Jerusalem" (clearly King Solomon) represents the epitome of wisdom, power, and the ability to gain what one desires, "for what will the man do who will come after the king except what has already been done?" (Eccl 2.12). If in Ecclesiastes the king himself despairs of finding authentic meaning and fulfillment from life's pleasures, then surely no one else can do so. Surely "all is vanity" (Eccl 1.2).

The royal figure of Solomon functions in the same way in the Song: if wealth, elegance, and power make one desirable, then surely no man could hope to be more desirable than the king. The Song celebrates every facet of human love, with its hidden roots and untapped possibilities, and not the experience of a particular human couple. It is anthropological celebration, not Solomonic autobiography. This being so, the mutual delight of any couple technically might have served the author's purpose, even two ordinary

[1]The Hebrew *le-Shlomo* may equally indicate that the song belongs to Solomon, as in a text commissioned by him, but written by another.

poor people. Indeed, our own affluent culture finds a certain unique romance in the union of hopelessly poor young lovers, with their poverty serving to accentuate the purity and glory of their love all the more. Would not such common people serve the author's purpose just as well? Such is not the case here, for the Song's celebration of the height of human love and delight demands that the lovers live at the height of human privilege and possibility. For a task so noble, only a king will do. However, as stated above, this is a fictive King Solomon, not the historical one, just as his partner is not a real historical person but a poetic creation. The Song is not about Solomon as a historical figure, but about the many and varied glories of love.

Reflection: The Significance of Solomon

Whether Solomon is present in the text as its author or sponsor, or as the creation of a later writer, a Christian cannot help but see him as a type of Christ. We find the roots of this typology in the Psalter. Interpreters often pair Psalm 45 with Psalm 72, with the latter designated "A Psalm of Solomon."[2] Indeed, both psalms describe a king in terms too grandiose to be applied to any lesser king of Israel, or perhaps even to the historical Solomon himself. The throne of the king in Psalm 45 is a divine one, and the psalmist addresses him in v. 6 as if he were divine: "Your throne, O God, is forever and ever."[3] The psalmist praises the king as a vindicator of righteousness: "Gird your sword on your thigh, O mighty one, in your splendor and your majesty, and in your majesty ride on victoriously in the cause of truth and meekness and righteousness" (Ps 45.3–4). He is also a person of wealth, for in ivory palaces stringed instruments make him glad with their music, and kings' daughters are among those of his harem (vv. 8–9).

---

[2] The Hebrew of course is "*le*-Solomon," containing the same ambiguity of translation as does Song 1.1; the Septuagint renders it Εἰς Σαλωμών, "Regarding Solomon" or perhaps "For Solomon."

[3] The inference of divinity remains, even if one adopts the translation "your divine throne endures forever and ever" (RSV).

The more explicitly Solomonic Psalm 72 continues this hyperbolic language. The king is again praised as a vindicator of righteousness: "He will judge your people with righteousness and your afflicted with justice. . . . He will vindicate the afflicted of the people, save the children of the needy, and crush the oppressor" (Ps 72.2, 4). These are not merely royal functions, but Messianic ones. The king's authority is indeed messianic, for "they will fear [him] while the sun endures and as long as the moon, throughout all generations" (v. 5). He will rule from sea to sea, from the Euphrates River to the ends of the earth. The nomads of the desert will bow before him, and the kings of Tarshish and of the distant islands will bring him gifts. Indeed all the kings will bow down before him, and all nations serve him (vv. 8–11). Everyone will bless themselves by him, and all nations will call him blessed (v. 17). While the psalm may be ascribed to Solomon, such poetry points beyond Solomon to the Messiah, the Christ of the House of David.

Given this established line connecting the historical Solomon and his glory to the Messiah, it was inevitable that Christians should see in the Solomon of the Song an image of Jesus, the bridegroom of the Church. Not only does human love point to the divine love, but the figure of Solomon already points to Christ. If the historical Solomon was famous for his wealth and wisdom (1 Kg 3.12–13), it is only in Christ that true and lasting riches and wisdom are to be found.

Christ does not simply bestow wealth; he *is* our wealth, the only truly enduring wealth that exists. Earthly riches may be stolen or corroded, for thieves break in and moth and rust destroy (Mt 6.19). The only riches safe from the changes and chances of time are the riches of immortality, which come to us as we put on Christ (Gal 3.27). Christ was rich, existing in the form of God, and yet for our sake became poor, emptying himself of heavenly glory in order to put on the form of a servant (Phil 2.6–7). Through his self-impoverishment he lifted us back to God, so that we might become rich through his poverty (2 Cor 8.9). The riches that he shares with us are the riches of immortality, of which we partake through our final union with him (1 Cor 15.53; 2 Pet 1.4). Solomon's vast wealth is thus a prophetic image of the boundless wealth of Christ and the goodness that he will bestow upon his people in the endless ages to come.

Solomon was also famous for his wisdom, as even the distant Queen of Sheba had heard (1 Kg 10.1f). Christ, however is not simply wise; he is wisdom itself, the eternal wisdom of God (1 Cor 1.30). In him are hidden all the treasures of wisdom and knowledge (Col 2.3). Where the author of Proverbs praises Wisdom as eternal, possessed by God at the beginning when there were neither depths nor water springs (Prov 8.22–24), Paul and those after him interpret this passage christologically, seeing in the eternal divine Wisdom a prophetic image of the Word. Christ is the divine wisdom, and just as we possess the wealth of immortality through him, so we also possess wisdom. Wisdom is the knowledge of God, a life-giving light that illumines all. Through our union with Christ our own hearts are illumined by that light, which fills us with the saving knowledge of God.

The presence of Solomon throughout the text therefore is prophetic, for he bears the image of the Church's bridegroom. As St Gregory of Nyssa says in his first homily on the Song:

> Do you suppose I am speaking of the Solomon from Beersheba ... ? Surely not! In this case, another Solomon is meant: the Solomon who "was born of the seed of David according to the flesh" (Rom 1:3), whose name is Peace, the true King of Israel, the builder of God's temple. . . . This Solomon used our Solomon as an instrument and by means of his voice speaks with us.[4]

---

[4]Gregory of Nyssa, *Homily* 1 (*GNO* 6:16–17). Translation in *Homilies*, 17, 19.

2

The Woman longs for the King's love (1.2–4)

The Woman:[1]

₁.₂Let him kiss me with the kisses of his mouth,
for your caresses[2] are better than wine!
₃Your anointing oils are fragrant,
your name is like purified[3] anointing oil;
therefore the maidens love you.
₄Draw me after you! We will make haste!
Let the king[4] bring me into his chambers!

The Chorus[5]:

₅We will exult in you and rejoice;
we will extol your caresses more than wine.
Rightly do they love you!

---

[1]Headings to indicate the speaker's traditional identity have been added for greater clarity. The identity of the speaker is not certain in every case.

[2]The Septuagint consistently vocalizes the Hebrew to read *dadim* (breasts) instead of *dodim* (caresses).

[3]Literally oil "emptied out," i.e., emptied from one vessel to another to purify it. The Septuagint Greek is ἐκκενωθὲν (*ekkenōthen*). Resemblance to the verb κενόω (*kenoō*), used to describe Christ's self-emptying in Phil 2.7, led some commentators to interpret the verb here as a reference to Christ's incarnation.

[4]We note in passing this evidence for the identification of the lover with Solomon. Given the superscription in 1.1 and the references to Solomon in 3.7f and 8.11f, attempts to make the title "king" refer to a fictive pet name, as in "You are a king to me," do not convince.

[5]The chorus fulfills a variety of functions throughout the Song, defying attempts to identify them as a stable, consistent group. Theirs is a poetic function, not a dramatic one. Here they represent the women of Jerusalem.

The Song opens with the voice of the bride. As the dominant person-
ality throughout the text, she has a majority of the poetic lines. This,
along with the absence of her father in the text, has led some feminist
writers to find in the Song the voice of an early feminist—a coun-
ter-cultural protest against the patriarchalism of the day.[6] While
this interpretation may seem anachronistic, there is no denying the
unusual emphasis on feminine sexual desire in the text, which stands
out all the more in the context of a culture where women were seen as
not taking the lead in marriage. Here, the woman begins the drama
of romance as the chief instigator.

The Song thus begins with her cry of desire, an erotic exclamation: "*Let him kiss me with the kisses of his mouth!*" Some uncertainty
is attached to what is meant by "the kisses of his mouth," with some
commentators[7] contrasting it to a less amorous "nose kiss." It seems
more likely that the bride is thinking of her beloved's mouth more
than she is of any contrasting kind of kiss. Her fervent desire is not
for a quick peck, but a long deep kiss, prelude to a night of lovemaking. This is apparent from her next words: "*for your caresses are better
than wine.*" (The shift from the third person to the second person is
typical of this lyric poetry in which delight defies grammar.) The
Hebrew word rendered here as *caresses* is plural, and so it demands
something more specific than generalized "love" (as translated by
the RSV, for example). *Caresses* refers to all the actions of lovemaking, one of which is the desired long, deep kiss. She can hardly
wait for such lovemaking, for she finds it *better*, more intoxicating
(Hebrew *tov*, good), *than wine*. Wine indeed makes glad the human
heart (Ps 104.15), but the King's lovemaking surpasses even this and
makes her giddy.

Not only does the woman long to taste her lover, but she delights
in his scent too: "*your anointing oils* [cologne] *are fragrant.*" And
such is the power of scent upon memory that very mention of his
name summons up her desire: his *name is like purified anointing*

[6]Surveyed by Exum, *Song of Songs,* 80–81.
[7]Snaith, *The Song of Songs,* 15, 108.

oil,[8] and the sound of it in her ears brings back the memory of his fragrance and their time together. That is why, she confesses, all the *maidens love* him, why every girl wants him for their own. In finding him, she has found the best. Her enthusiasm for her lover makes her impatient, and she again cries out, "*Draw me after you! We will make haste!*" Longing to find a place of privacy for their intimacy, she cries, "*Let the king bring me into his chambers*," his private rooms. The scene draws to a discreet close with the words of the poetic chorus, as they *exult* and *rejoice* over the lovers. They too know that the king's *caresses* are to be extolled *more than wine*, so that the maidens *rightly love* him. The term *rightly* here has the sense of naturally, inevitably. The king is so wonderful, how could all the girls not love him?

Reflection: The Priority of the Woman and Her Desire

Many commentators have noted that throughout the Song it is the woman who takes priority, not the man. The Song focuses more on the bride than upon the bridegroom. As mentioned above, she has the majority of the lines, and she is the first and the last to speak (1.2, 8.14). Though the couple competes in trading compliments and praising each other, hers is the voice of the most fervent longing. She is the one who goes searching throughout the streets of the city for him and not vice versa; she is the one who swoons (5.6) and who longs for his love during his absence. Though it is apparent from his speeches that he is smitten with her (see 4.9, 6.5), hers is the stronger voice, the voice of the greatest desire. What is the deeper significance of this?

If in the voice of the woman we can detect the voice of the bride of Christ, then her prominence in the Song and her desire express the importance of desire for God in the experience of salvation. Her passionate longing for *the kisses of his mouth*, for his *caresses*, and her *haste* to follow after him into the privacy of *his chambers* (that is, her intense desire to experience him as fully as possible) all witness to

[8]The words contain a wordplay: "Your *shem* (name) is like *shemen* (anointing oil)."

the soul's desire for God, its thirst for truth, beauty, and goodness. This thirst forms the foundation for all spirituality, for without it religious experience is either prideful delusion or empty ritual. This is why, in the continuing dialogue between the lovers, the woman is the first to speak: individual salvation begins with this spiritual thirst, this cry of the heart for God.

St Gregory of Nyssa recognized how culturally unusual it was to focus upon the desire of the woman for the man. In his first homily, he writes that the Song "does not, after the human custom, take the bridegroom's desire as its starting point. Ahead of the bridegroom it presents the virgin who is blamelessly giving voice to her desire and praying that she may at some time savor the bridegroom's kiss."[9]

Our saving relationship with God begins with this cry. We hear this cry on the day of Pentecost, when three thousand of Peter's hearers are cut to the heart and cry out, "Brethren, what shall we do?" (Acts 2.37). We hear it in the cry of the Philippian jailer when he says to Paul and Silas, "Sirs, what must I do to be saved?" (Acts 16.30). We even catch its echo in the searching question of the rich young ruler when he says to Christ, "All these things [that you command me] I have kept; what am I still lacking?" (Mt 19.20). This last example reveals that thirst and the experience of lack alone do not guarantee that the soul will pay the price necessary to slake its thirst and fill the void. But clearly without this thirst and recognition of lack, no one can truly experience salvation.

We see this thirst depicted throughout the Psalter. Thus, the cry of the psalmist in Psalm 42.1–2: "As the deer longs for the water brooks, so my soul longs for you, O God. My soul thirsts for God, for the living God; when shall I come and appear before God?" And thus the cry of Psalm 63.1: "O God, you are my God; I shall seek you early. My souls thirsts for you, my flesh faints for you in a dry and weary land where there is no water." Or that cry of Psalm 84.1–2: "How lovely are your dwelling places, O Lord of hosts! My soul longed and even yearned for the courts of the Lord; my heart and

[9]Gregory of Nyssa, Homily 1 (GNO 6:23–24). Translation in Homilies, 25.

my flesh sing for joy to the living God." These cries are not expressed in the erotic language of the bride, such as we find in the Song, but they are equally fervent and even desperate cries of desire. In them we hear not just the voice of the psalmist but also the very voice of the Church—and of every soul in whose heart are the highways to Zion. As Gregory of Nyssa says concerning this passage, "Just as now the soul that is joined to God is not satiated by her enjoyment of him, so too the more abundantly she is filled up with his beauty, the more vehemently her longings abound."[10] The soul's constant and increasing longing for God finds expression in the Song's opening verses, and in them we see the first steps of the soul's journey to God.

It is true of course that salvation begins with God, with the love of the heavenly bridegroom, and not with man. God's plan for his bride was formed before the foundation of the world (Eph 1.4), for while we were still sinners Christ died for us (Rom 5.8). His love has priority, and we love only in response to him; we love because he first loved us (1 John 4.19). That is all true, but it is not the message of the Song. The Song delves into the depths of the redeemed heart, plotting and mapping the way back to God. Since its focus is exclusively experiential, it gives priority to the need of the bride for her bridegroom. Our salvation begins when we recognize our spiritual poverty, our need for God's love, for God's rescue. It begins with an expression of spiritual thirst and desperate longing for him. For this reason it is difficult for the wealthy to enter the kingdom of God: their riches distract them, smothering the thirst for God that lies deep in the center of every human being. The rich believe that they need nothing (Rev 3.17), and in them the hunger for truth is dead. They have filled their bellies with the husks that swine eat (Lk 15.16), and thus have no desire for the true food that only the Father can provide in his house. Salvation becomes possible only when inner hunger awakens, and we feel our absence from God like a pain burning in the belly.

[10]Ibid., 33.

The woman in the Song feels this pain, and knows that peace can only come when she experiences the presence of her lover. That is why the first words of the Song are words of desperate desire.

3

The Woman seeks the King among his flock (1.5–2.7)

The Woman:

1.5Dark I am, but lovely,
O daughters of Jerusalem,
like the tents of Kedar,
like the curtains of Solomon.
6Do not stare at me because I am swarthy,
for the sun has looked down on me.
My mother's sons[1] were angry with me;
they made me keeper of the vineyards,
but my own vineyard I have not kept.

The poetry continues with a revelation of the woman's vulnerability—a potent part of any woman's attractiveness in men's eyes. In particular she confesses that she is *dark* (literally, black). The image is of someone *swarthy*, dark as the black *tents of Kedar*. Kedar refers to the Bedouin tribes of Arabia who lived in tents made of black goat hair. This dark complexion, she explains, was caused by her long hours working in the family *vineyards*, where *the sun looked down* on her, burning her skin and giving her a deep suntan. Adding to the pathos of her plight is the cause of her long hours laboring

[1]Some commentators suggest the phrase indicates that the men were stepbrothers, not full brothers, for the normal designation for full brothers would be "my *father's* sons," not "my mother's sons." But it is equally possible that the phrase is meant simply to stress the close connection of the men with herself, and thus emphasize the injustice of their oppression.

under the burning sun: "*My mother's sons were angry at me*" and so forced her to work for them—even to the point of neglecting her *own vineyard* and suffering personal deprivation. The biographical details of the situation are irrelevant, however, and should not be pressed. Asking questions such as "Why were they angry at her? Was it because they thought she was too sexually free?"[2] misses the point. She is a Cinderella figure, unjustly forced to labor under the hot sun by her powerful brothers, who for some unknown reason were causing her grief.

Because her swarthy complexion might cause some to disdain her, she tells *the daughters of Jerusalem* not to *stare* at her, nor regard her as unworthy of the king. Despite her dark complexion, she is still *lovely*; she may resemble the black tents of Kedar, but also the exquisite *curtains of Solomon*, the tent curtains of the king. (Not, of course, that Solomon literally dwelt in a tent, but the poetic contrast is made between the dwellings of the king and the Bedouins of Kedar.)

Why, we may wonder today, would her dark complexion be considered a problem by some people? The issue was not racial, but economic. Despite the desire of some modern readers to find here a woman of African race (and thus make the Song a celebration of interracial marriage),[3] it seems clear that this woman is a local girl, since her brothers own vineyards in the approximate area. Rather than racial discrimination, the concern is that she comes from the lower classes that had to labor in the sun to survive, rather than from the wealthier, more refined families of Jerusalem.

Our own culture regards tanned skin as desirable, but in that day a suntan represented long hard hours of manual labor and was regarded as a sign that a girl was a mere peasant, someone who could never aspire to a royal marriage. The girl protests this evaluation: she may be dark, but she is lovely. She is no mere peasant, ugly and prematurely aged by a life of backbreaking toil and grinding poverty.

---

[2]As suggested in Gordis, *The Song of Songs and Lamentations* (New York: KTAV Publishing House, 1974), 46.

[3]Garrett, *Song of Songs*, 133.

She is noble, and correspondingly beautiful. If she appears dark, it is only because the sun has stared at her during her long hours in the vineyard; let not the daughters of Jerusalem stare disapprovingly, too. She is no peasant but merely a victim of her family, and thus it would be better to offer sympathy instead of disdain. Under her recently acquired suntan, she is still radiant and fit for a king.

Reflection: Apologizing for Appearance

After the opening poem, the woman immediately hastens to declare her defect: a swarthiness of skin caused by the relentless ray of the sun. She is concerned that this swarthiness may cause her to be disdained as a poor peasant, someone whose youth and beauty has been worn away by years of toil, making her unfit for the king. And so she protests that her darkness has its origin in her oppression by her brothers and not in her economic status.

The issue of dark skin raises the question of her suitability for a union with the king. A life of poverty that stamps wear and tear onto a girl's features, disfiguring her youthful beauty, would surely disqualify a girl from such a union. The beauty and radiance that come as the fruit of wealth, on the other hand, qualify her as a possible mate for the king—that is why the woman says that although she is *dark*, she is also *lovely*, explaining her swarthiness as a temporary result of working in the *vineyards* of her *mother's sons*.

If we transpose the woman's protest and explanation into the context of our union with God, we see what truly disqualifies us from that saving relationship. The darkness of sin cannot disqualify us; only a hard and impenitent heart can do so. The woman's dark complexion offers an image of the darkness of sin, telling us that our sinful misdeeds darken us internally. As Gregory of Nyssa says in his second homily on this passage, the burning and darkening sun is a symbol for "the hostile assault of temptation and trial."[4] Just as a life of grinding poverty can disfigure one's features and rob the young of

[4]Gregory of Nyssa, *Homily* 2 (*GNO* 6:51). Translation in *Homilies*, 57.

their beauty, so a life full of impenitence and rebellion can disfigure our souls. We can never approach union with Christ in that state. So long as we retain the inner beauty of a heart that mourns its sin and travels on the royal road of repentance, we are still fit for the King. We may be dark, having endured passing wounds from the hostile assault of temptation and trial. But these wounds will eventually heal, even as the swarthiness of skin burnt by the sun will also pass. What matters—and what allows us to aspire to a royal union with our Lord—is the humble and contrite heart that breaks over its sin (Ps 51.17).

> *The Woman*:
>
> ₁.₇Tell me, O you whom my soul loves,
> where do you pasture?
> Where do you cause your flock to lie down at noon?
> For why should I be like one who veils herself
> beside the flocks of your companions?

The woman now turns from defending herself to the daughters of Jerusalem and addresses her beloved directly. She addresses her lover as if he were a shepherd, pasturing his flock along with the other shepherds. Once again we perceive the error of reading the text as if it were biography and raising the question of why the king would do the humble work of a shepherd. The king was not a shepherd, nor did he actually pasture his flocks. The lover as shepherd pasturing his flock is a poetic image that conjures up an idyllic pastoral setting for the sake of emotional romance. This image is made all the more natural by the fact that in Scripture, kings and rulers are often referred to as shepherds (cf. Ezek 34).

The woman asks her lover to *tell* her where he *pastures* his flock, and where he makes them *lie down at noon*. During the noonday hours a shepherd would often take his flock to a cool, sheltered place and rest until the heat of the day had subsided. She longs to join him there, no doubt to lie down with him even as he makes his flock lie down. Where can they meet? At what place can they make their secret tryst? Let him tell her, she begs, lest she be forced to go about with the other shepherds, among *the flocks of* his *companions*, asking after him. Such behavior would scarcely be proper, for she would resemble *one who veils herself*, that is, a prostitute, one who goes about where the men are, soliciting partners (see Gen 38.15). Therefore she asks him, "Where can I find you?"

> *The Man:*
>
> 1.8If you yourself do not know,
> O fairest among women,
> go forth in the footsteps of the flock
> and pasture your kids
> by the tents of the shepherds.
> 9To me, my companion, you are like
> my mare among the chariots of Pharaoh.
> 10Your cheeks are lovely with pendants,
> your neck with necklaces.
> 11We will make for you pendants of gold
> with beads of silver.

His reply to her entreaties is teasing. Instead of revealing where he intends to pasture his flock (and therefore where she might meet him), he simply replies, "*Go forth in the footsteps of the flock and pasture your kids* (i.e., young goats) *by the tents of the shepherds*"—in other words, "Come follow us and find out." He wants her to pursue him, to enjoy the chase. For all of the dialogue's erotic intensity, the element of playfulness has not been excluded. One finds such an element of playful chase in many of the great romances—hence the common experience immortalized in the line from the Irving Berlin song "a man chases a girl until she catches him."

However, he quickly returns to lose himself in her loveliness. The metaphors used throughout the Song are timely, meaning that they savor of their time, not ours. Some of the metaphors make little romantic sense to us now, including the first compliment the lover pays his beloved, for he compares her to his *mare among the chariots of Pharaoh*. The king's comparison of his beloved to his *mare* among those horses made more romantic sense at the time, for horses were associated with royalty rather than with the common tasks of farming and transport. He looks at his love and is impressed with her bearing: she is dignified, regal, and magnificent, like his royal mare.

In particular the king praises her *cheeks* (face) and *neck*, for both are *lovely with pendants* (or possibly "earrings") and *necklaces*. Note the modesty of this first descriptive praise, for he praises only the parts of her that he can see, her face and neck. He looks at the orna-ments that adorn her and wants to provide her with even richer gifts, *pendants of gold* and *beads of silver*. (The plural *we* refers to those subjects through whom the king procures such treasures.) Such regal nobility demands suitable adornment. One can almost see the king stroking her face and neck, lost in admiration of her beauty. The lover's first words are characterized by elegance and restraint. There is nothing carnal, lewd, or aggressive; the king is also a gentleman.

Reflection: Searching for the Shepherd

In this romantic vignette we observe the classic element of the play-ful chase, wherein the woman expresses her desire to meet her lover for a quiet tryst in the middle of the day, while he refuses to divulge his future whereabouts, urging her to come and find him for herself. This element of chase is of course part of the erotic buildup, since her desire for him grows as she looks for him, just as he intended. Despite the carefree and light-hearted character of this vignette, we find here theological insights regarding our own relationship with the Lord.

The element of pursuit—or, more accurately, of seeking and gradual approach—is present in our approach to Christ as well. Its classic Scriptural formulation is in the first chapter of John's Gospel. There we read that Christ turned around to find two of John the Baptist's disciples following him. He asks them, "What do you seek?" When they reply, "Rabbi, where are you staying?" he responds, "Come and you will see" (Jn 1.38–39). Just as the approach of the two disciples was a gradual one, so Christ does not reveal himself fully to his inquirers all at once. First came a time of seeking and waiting, which served to test their sincerity. Did they really want to find the truth? Then let them come and search for it.

This gradual approach is reproduced in the soul of everyone who would find Christ and convert to faith in him. First one hears the gospel, perhaps through a friend or through reading Christian literature. Then one comes to church and is exposed to the power of the liturgical assembly. One begins to turn over in one's own mind what this all could mean and whether one should commit oneself to Christ. A change as momentous as conversion takes time. The decision to give one's life to Christ cannot be quickly made, if it is to last. It requires extended thought and a gradual approach. One needs time to count the cost (Lk 14.28) and to gather up one's whole life in order to entrust it to Christ.

That is why the early Church instituted the catechumenate: to facilitate such conversions. This period of preparation classically lasted three years—a gradual approach indeed, but intended to foster fervent desire for Christ and the Eucharist in the soul of the convert. Even today many converts testify that their time in the catechumenate gave them an appreciation for church membership and their inclusion in the Eucharist that they might not have gained otherwise.

The soul's approach to Christ must always contain an element of searching, and not only during the initial time of conversion. Love for Christ constitutes a continual search, a pilgrimage and journey ever deeper into the kingdom of God, and ever further from the

fallen things of the world. Proverbs 2.1ff bids us seek for wisdom as
if it were a hidden treasure of silver, to lift up our voices and beg for
it. In Jeremiah 29.13, God tells us that if we seek him we will find him,
but only if we search for him with all our heart. This is the fervent
search of the woman for her king, her journey in the *footsteps of the
flock*, her determination to find the one *whom* her *soul loves* and *lie
down* with him *at noon*. It is the abiding paradox of discipleship: having found Christ we continue to seek him in our hearts, pressing ever
onward with him into his kingdom. The soul's progress in holiness
and inner beauty is reflected in the shepherd's offer to beautify the
woman even further. Her *cheeks* are already *lovely with pendants* and
her *neck with necklaces*. But he would beautify them even further,
replacing and supplementing her jewelry with *pendants of gold* and
beads of silver. If her search for the shepherd is successful, she will
find access to even greater beauty by finding him.

> *The Woman*:
>
> 1.12While the king was on his couch,
> my nard gave forth its fragrance.
> 13My beloved is to me a pouch of myrrh,
> which lies all night between my breasts.
> 14My beloved is to me a cluster of henna blossoms
> in the vineyards of En-gedi.

The woman, responding with greater suggestivity and an elegance
suffused with passion, offers the first of the many double entendres
found in the Song. She expresses the mutuality of their delight
through the image of fragrance: *while the king lies on his couch*, her
feelings are aroused so that her *nard gives forth its fragrance*. Nard
or spikenard, also called muskroot, was a form of lavender so costly
and highly valued in the ancient world as to be found only among
the wealthy. (In New Testament times, a vial of it could cost three
hundred denarii, almost a year's wages for the working man; Mk

14.5.) Here, it expresses her desire. It is unlikely that she would actually have worn such nard, but she describes the sexual gift she has to offer in the most glowing of terms.

Her *beloved* also is fragrant, smelling like *myrrh*, an aromatic gum used in incense and to perfume garments (Ps 45.8). Indeed, she describes him as *a pouch of myrrh which lies all night between her breasts*—an apt image, since that is in fact where he lay all night. Once again, note that she is not suggesting that she actually wore pulverized myrrh in a sachet on a thong between her breasts as a source of perfume. She is describing her lover, not her clothing. He is as potent to her senses as myrrh would be, filling her head with its overpowering fragrance.

The combined imagery draws its potency from the power of the sense of smell as the lovers, each adorned with powerful perfume, combine their fragrances as they lie entwined on the couch. Nard and myrrh flow together to become a single intoxicating fragrance. The woman compounds the olfactory metaphors, repeating how fragrant, i.e., how desirable, her beloved is—he is also *a cluster of henna blossoms in the vineyards of En-gedi*. En-gedi, meaning "spring of the wild goats," was a lush oasis west of the Dead Sea, famous for its tropical climate and the fertility of its gardens. The henna that grew there was strongly scented, smelling (some said) of roses. The woman multiplies the images of fragrance so as to say that her lover smells of myrrh and henna, distracting and overpowering.

Reflection: The Scent of Holiness

We come now to the first of many references to fragrance in the Song, as the woman declares that being with the *king on his couch* causes her own *nard* to *give forth its fragrance*—that is, it caused her own desire to flow. This image leads to other images that depict her lover as *a pouch of myrrh* and *a cluster of henna blossoms*. He also is fragrant with desire, which in turn awakens her desire all the more.

There are many other references to fragrance throughout the text. Thus we find references to the fragrance of apples in 2.3–5 and 7.8; to the vines in blossom spreading their fragrance in 2.13; to myrrh, frankincense, and the powders of the merchant in 3.6; scented lilies in 4.5, 5.13, 6.2–3, and 7.2; a mountain of myrrh and a hill of frankincense in 4.6; the fragrance of anointing oils in 4.10; fragrant garments in 4.11; the combined odors of henna blossoms, nard plants, saffron, calamus, cinnamon, frankincense, myrrh, aloe, and all the chief spices in 4.13–14; myrrh in 5.1, liquid myrrh in 5.5, 5.13; beds of spices in 6.2, and a mountain of spices in 8.14. When these are taken together the text is almost overwhelmed with fragrance, made all the more potent by the role of the sense of smell in arousing memory.

Such a profusion of images cannot be theologically insignificant. Indeed, we find beautiful fragrance as a metaphor for sanctity throughout the Scriptures. Building upon the primitive concept that the gods enjoyed the smell of the sacrifices, the narrative in Genesis relates that after the flood Noah offered a sacrifice to God. When "the Lord smelled the soothing aroma," he said, "I will never again curse the ground on account of man" (Gen 8.20–21). We should not regard Noah's God as actually enjoying the smell of roasting meat; the cultural associations of smell provide the material for the metaphor. Because of the importance of smell in the ancient world, incense became an essential part of the worship of God—instructions for its preparation are found in Exodus 30.34–38—and came to symbolize the acceptability of prayer and worship (Ps 141.2; Rev 8.3–4).

Paul continued in this tradition when he wrote to the Corinthians that the apostles were "a fragrance of Christ to God" both "among those who are being saved and among those who are perishing"; to the latter they are "an aroma from death to death" and to the former "an aroma from life to life" (2 Cor 2.15–16). The fragrance or presence of Christ lingering upon the apostles was for the early Christians an odor of sanctity, betokening abundant life. Paul also speaks of Christ's death as "a sacrifice to God, as a fragrant aroma"

(Eph 5.2), and calls the gift that the Philippians gave him "a fragrant aroma, an acceptable sacrifice, well pleasing to God" (Phil 4.18).

This consistent connection of fragrance with holiness allows us to see, in the references to fragrance throughout the Song, an image of sanctity, goodness, and spiritual beauty. It is significant that *both* the lovers are suffused with this fragrance: he is a pouch of myrrh, a cluster of henna blossoms, while she possesses the fragrance of nard. Indeed, when they are together their fragrances coalesce and combine, becoming a single overpowering scent. This mutuality of fragrance speaks of the union that Christ has with his church, and with the individual believers within it. We find within the Church a single fragrance of life, a single scent, a single holiness, as the holiness of Christ the Head flows down to his members. In the Church there is only one who is fragrant, only one who is holy, only one who is the Lord—Jesus Christ, to the glory of God the Father.[5] All our fragrance and holiness come from him. These words in the Song encourage us to spend time with the Lord in prayer and liturgy, that the fragrance of his presence might mingle with ours and preserve in us the scent of holiness.

> *The Man*:
>
> 1.15Behold, how fair you are, my companion,
> behold, how fair you are!
> Your eyes are doves.

> *The Woman*:
>
> 16Behold, how fair you are, my beloved,
> and so delightful!
> Indeed, our couch is luxuriant!
> 17The beams of our houses are cedars,
> our rafters, cypresses.

[5]From the elevation of the Lamb at the Orthodox Divine Liturgy [the people's response to the priest's words, "The holy things are for the holy"—*Ed.*].

As the lovers exchange compliments, we can almost see them gazing into each other's eyes. The man says to his beloved, "Behold, how fair you are, my companion," repeating it twice. The compliment is preceded both times by *behold*, an expression of surprise, as if he cannot believe what he is seeing or his good fortune in having found her. It corresponds to the exclamation "Ah!" in English, a cry of surprised appreciation. He gazes into her eyes, announcing, "Your eyes are doves." The exact point of the metaphor is not clear—does he refer to the shape of her eyes (large and luminous), their color (smoke grey), their delicacy, or perhaps to the gentleness of her gaze? The poetry does not compel us to choose, and perhaps he means all of them. Doves were commonly regarded as messengers of love, and he can see her love for him reflected in her eyes.

Gazing back into his eyes, the woman echoes his words: "Behold, how fair you are!" Being with him is *delightful*, especially when they lie together: their *couch* is *luxuriant*. The word rendered here as *luxuriant* is the Hebrew word for green, and from the references that follow to *the beams of* their *houses* being *cedars* and their *rafters, cypresses*, it is clear that they are in an outdoor garden with trees. Their place of trysting apparently offers many places in which to lie, for the woman speaks of *houses* in the plural. The lovers find privacy outdoors in a bucolic and idyllic natural setting, shaded by the trees.

The Woman:

2.1I am a flower of the plain,
a lily of the valleys.

The Man:

2Like a lily among the thorns,
so is my companion among the daughters.

The Woman:

3Like an apple tree among the trees of the forest,

> so is my beloved among the sons.
> I rested with delight in his shade,[6]
> and his fruit was sweet to my palate.
> ₄He brought me to his banquet hall,
> and his banner over me was love.
> ₅Sustain me with raisin-cakes,
> refresh me with apples,
> for I am faint with love.
> ₆Let his left hand be under my head
> and his right hand embrace me.
> ₇I adjure you, O daughters of Jerusalem,
> by the gazelles or by the does of the field,
> that you do not arouse or awaken the love
> until he pleases.

The woman continues her dialogue with her lover. After telling him that he is fair and delightful (1.16), she opines that she herself is nobody special. Indeed, she is as ordinary as *a flower of the plain*, a mere *lily of the valleys*. This description, better known in its more classical rendering as "the rose of Sharon," has been understood to be the woman's boast about her beauty. This rendering, however, cannot be sustained. Firstly, the plant we recognize as a rose was not present in the Holy Land in that day. The Hebrew word *chabatselet* is impossible to identify with certainty, while the Greek word used to render it in the Septuagint is *anthos* (ἄνθος), which means simply "blossom," or any wildflower whose blossoms quickly fade (thus its use in James 1.11, 1 Peter 1.24). Also, the classic rendering "the rose of Sharon" refers to the low coastal plain of Sharon in the north of the Holy Land (*sharon* means "plain"), whereas both the Hebrew and the Greek Septuagint refer to "*the* sharon." The latter text translates the title as "a flower" (τοῦ πεδίου, *tou pediou*) of the plain. This parallels the title that follows: a lily *of the valleys*. Which plain or valley is

2.1

---

[6]Literally, "in his shade I desired and I sat," sitting being an image of rest, rather than a particular posture. The verb is sometimes rendered "dwelt," e.g., Gen 37.1, to indicate staying in a place for a long time.

meant becomes irrelevant; the woman's point is that she resembles a wildflower that can be found growing in abundance in any plain or valley. She does not believe it, of course, but merely offers self-deprecation so that her lover will contradict her—which he quickly does.

Indeed, her lover jumps in to say that if she would call herself a lily of the valleys, then she is *a lily among the thorns*. Her beauty surpasses the beauty of the other girls (*the daughters*) as the beauty of a lily surpasses that of surrounding thorns.

The woman is not slow to return the compliment. If she is a lily among thorns, then he is like *an apple tree among the trees of the forest*, as superior to the other men (*the sons*) as a fruit tree would be compared to surrounding trees that bore no fruit. The Hebrew word usually rendered "apple" need not be an apple; some translations, such as the New English Bible, render it as "apricot." The precise identification does not matter; the woman praises her lover as a source of pleasure, with *his fruit* being *sweet to* her *palate*. (Apples, like apricots, are not simply food, but pleasing, aromatic, refreshing, and sensuous.) So pleasing is her lover that she *rested with delight in his shade*, enjoying his company, tasting his fruit. While the metaphor is one of resting under a shady fruit tree for a time and eating its fruit, the corresponding reality is of course sexual.

This meaning is apparent from the woman's next words, for the poetry now switches from direct address to a first-person reminiscence: *He brought me to his banquet hall, and his banner over me was love*. The phrase rendered here as *banquet hall* literally means "house of wine," and can thus refer to any place where wine is drunk. Although the term conveys an impression of a public banquet with others present, the location could equally well be a private chamber, or might even refer not so much to an actual place as to the experience of drinking wine together. More difficult to interpret is the phrase *his banner over me was love*. The word rendered as *banner* is the Hebrew word *degel*, which is the same word used in Numbers 2.3, where it refers to the military standards denoting the different tribes. Its use here seems to denote the woman's delight at having been conquered by him (though, as she stresses, the conquest was not carried out for the glory of any tribe, but for the glory of love). This being so, it seems more likely that the *banquet hall* where they drank wine together was occupied by themselves alone—perhaps their verdant trysting place under the cypresses (1.17).

We are given a last glimpse of the couple with the woman's plea that she be *sustained with raisin-cakes* and *refreshed with apples* (both of these foods of luxury were commonly thought to be aphrodisiacs), for she is *faint with love* and desire for her lover. She asks here for the strength to continue lovemaking, asking also that his *left hand be under* her *head and his right hand embrace* her. That is, we see them lying down together with him to her right, with his *left hand* (or arm) under her head and *his right hand* (or arm) pulling her close in an embrace. With this bold and vivid image the poetic curtain falls, concealing the lovers from our literary view.

The woman's next words are not addressed to the man, but rather to the *daughters of Jerusalem*. Clearly she has something of importance to say just before the curtain falls, for she does not make a simple request but rather *adjures* them, placing them under oath. It is an odd kind of oath, for she swears not by God but *by the gazelles or by the does of the field*. And what she demands of the daughters is that they *do not arouse or awaken the love until he pleases*.

This verse has occasioned all kinds of different interpretations and even different translations. Should the final phrase be rendered *until he pleases*[7] or until "it" pleases[8] perhaps even "until she pleases"?[9] Some interpreters[10] regard this verse as a plea not to rush passion or arouse desire prematurely, but to let it come in its own time. But here it is clear that the passion has long since begun. With the lovers already locked in a hot nuptial embrace, it makes no sense for one of them to stop and adjure the other girls to let the lovers take their time. Clearly, their time has come.

[7] Thus the authorized King James Version.
[8] The meaning assumed by the Jerusalem Bible.
[9] Thus the New American Standard Bible.
[10] Exum, *Song of Songs*, 117–118.

Some of the interpreters understand this verse as an exhortation to the women of Jerusalem not to rush love in general, offering them a sage bit of practical advice for their own lives (thus, the New American Bible rendering, "Do not stir up love before its own time"). According to one interpreter, the woman here "warns the others not to arouse love until they are ready to meet its rigors, both physical and emotional."[11] But such a moralistic maxim seems psychologically awkward in this place, so much so as to be virtually impossible. In the two other places where the adjuration is found in the Song (3.5, 8.4), it also follows immediately after the anticipated consummation of love. Are we really to believe that the woman, just before the curtain falls upon the two lovers passionately consummating their love, would disentangle herself and take time to offer to the other girls a timely word about hasty marriages? The intensity of the moment makes such an interpretation unlikely in the extreme. Other commentators[12] have interpreted the verse as representing a kind of "do not disturb" sign, as in "do not disturb lovemaking until it wishes to be disturbed." This fits well enough psychologically with the flow of the poetic narrative, but it is doubtful that the verbs *arouse* and *awaken* can be made to mean "disturb."

I suggest therefore that the woman, just before the narrative curtain falls, adjures her friends not to arouse or awaken her lover's passion, but to let him sleep. After the lovemaking he surely will fall asleep, and they must not wake him prematurely. The word *love* used here (Hebrew *ahabah*) is not a pet name for her beloved (that would be the Hebrew word *dodi*), but the general word for love also found in Song 2.4, 3.10, and 8.7. It is here prefaced by the definite article, *the love*, and not a possessive ("my" love). The woman insists that when he awakes his passion will awake with him, and the others must not arouse that passion prematurely by waking him up. The woman more or less identifies her beloved with his *love*.

[11]Tremper Longman III, *Song of Songs* (Grand Rapids, MI: Wm. B. Eerdmans Publishing Company, 2001), 116.

[12]Ibid., 115.

Also puzzling is the form of the oath she proposes, one sworn *by the gazelles or by the does of the field*. Some[13] have noticed that the Hebrew word for *gazelles* sounds similar to the Hebrew word for "hosts," as in "the Lord of Hosts," while the Hebrew for *does of the field* sounds similar to the Hebrew name God Almighty (*El Shaddai*). They suggest that these phrases are substitutes for the name of God. There is a similarity in the sounds, but one wonders why the poet would mention the form of the oath at all if he wanted to avoid mentioning the name of God in the poem. The woman might have said, "I adjure you," and left it at that. Why mention gazelles and deer? I suggest that the oath takes this form to highlight the pastoral setting of their lovemaking. If the lovers are indeed still among the cedars and cypresses (1.17), then the presence of gazelles and does can be expected as a feature of their outdoor tryst. Nothing would be more natural than for them to form part of the woman's adjuration as she loved and rested under the trees.

Reflection: Discipleship as Divine Dialogue

In the beginning of this section we see the first of many dialogues between the two lovers. In 1.15 the man addresses the woman, saying to her, "Behold, how fair you are, my companion, behold, how fair you are!" She then responds to him in turn, using almost the same words, "Behold, how fair you are, my beloved, and so delightful! I am a flower of the plain, a lily of the valleys." To this he responds by taking her own words about being a mere *lily of the valleys*, saying that if she is a lily, then she is *a lily among the thorns*, better than all the other *daughters*. She responds with a superlative compliment of her own, insisting that he is like a fragrant and tasty *apple tree among the* lesser *trees of the forest*, better than all the other *sons*. This back-and-forth trading of compliments is not the only time we find the lovers in dialogue with each other in the Song. In 4.16, the woman invites her lover to come into the garden and eat its fruit; in

[13]Longman, *Song of Songs*, 116.

5.1 he accepts her invitation to enter the garden and eat. The Song and its dialogues consist mostly of the lovers' mutual praise.

This in turn reflects an aspect of our discipleship with our Lord. Like all living relationships, our faith in Christ involves a kind of dialogue with him wherein he speaks through Scripture, conscience, and liturgy, and we respond in prayer. We do not offer up our life to him as if to a mute and distant deity, hoping he will ultimately reveal himself and have mercy on us at the end. Christ speaks to our hearts even now, and throughout our life gives us assurance of salvation and leads us along the path of continual transformation.

In this respect our faith differs from Islam. Islam teaches that no one can know God personally, for Allah remains transcendent, exalted, and distant from his servants. Islam asserts that one can know God's will through the Qur'an, but not him personally. It is otherwise with the Christian faith: through the Holy Spirit we can know Christ himself as we continually seek him through prayer, Scripture-reading, and sacrament. Obviously there is always the possibility of self-delusion and even *prelest*—the prideful insistence that what we experience is from God when in fact it has its origin in our own silly heads. But the possibility of prelest does not in the least invalidate the truth that the humble heart can actually come to know Christ himself and experience him. Jesus is not simply an historical figure, withdrawn now from us into a distant heaven, held incommunicado in his seat at God's right hand. On the contrary, his ascension makes him all the more accessible to every human heart that seeks him in humility. We can actually know the one who once walked by the shores of Galilee; indeed, our Christian life consists of that saving knowledge and dialogue. We do not simply believe the proposition that God exists and that Jesus of Nazareth was his Son; we actually experience the living God through his Son present in our midst. As C. S. Lewis once wrote, "*Credere Deum esse* [believing God exists] turns into *Credere in Deum* [believing in God]. And *Deum* here is this God, the increasingly knowable Lord."[14]

[14]C. S. Lewis, "On Obstinacy of Belief," in *They Asked for a Paper* (London: Geoffrey Bles, 1962), 196.

4

The Man comes to the home of his beloved (2.8–17)

The Woman:

2.8The voice of my beloved!
Behold, he is coming,
leaping over the mountains,
bounding over the hills!
9My beloved is like a gazelle or a young stag.
Behold, he is standing behind our wall,
he is looking through the windows,
he is peeking through the lattice.
10My beloved answered and said to me,
"Arise, my companion, my fair one,
and come!
11For lo, the winter is past,
the rain is over and gone.
12The blossoms appear in the earth;
the time of singing[1] has arrived,
and the voice of the turtledove has been heard in
    our land.
13The fig tree has ripened its fruit,[2]

[1]The verb could also mean "pruning" (thus the Septuagint); the more exuberant rendering seems a better fit for the context. Also, this reading allows the "time of singing" to be parallel to the "voice of the turtledove," the "singing" being that of the birds. This also preserves a kind of *chiasmus*, consisting of blossoms-singing of birds-voice of the turtledove-blossoming fig and vines.

[2]Literally, "has spiced [sweetened] its unripe figs."

and the vines in blossom have spread their fragrance.
Arise, my companion, my fair one,
and come!
₁₄O my dove, in the clefts of the rock,
in the covert of the cliff,
let me see your form, let me hear your voice;
for your voice is sweet,
and your form is lovely.
₁₅Catch the foxes for us,
the little foxes that are ruining the vineyards,
for our vineyards are in blossom."
₁₆My beloved is mine, and I am his;
he pastures among the lilies.
₁₇When the day breathes and the shadows flee,
turn, my beloved, and be like a gazelle
or a young stag on the cleft mountains.[3]

The scene now shifts, and her lover is gone. But he is not gone from her heart, and she longs to be with him again. In this new scene, the woman hears *the voice of* her *beloved* and leaps up in excited anticipation of his visit. She imagines him *coming* nearer to her in her house, *leaping over the mountains, bounding over the hills*, traversing great distances to be with him like a strong and lively *gazelle or a young stag*. The image is of her lover coming to her at her family home, calling her name as he draws ever nearer. At last *he is standing behind our wall* (the plural "our" identifies the wall as part of her family's residence) he then comes closer, *looking through the windows*, and *peeking through the lattice*, eager for a sight of his beloved, whose name he is doubtless still calling. The narration of his gradual approach mirrors her growing desire for his arrival and presence.

As he looks for a sight of his beloved through the windows and lattices of their house, he *answered* her. Why "*answered*"? What has she said to which he can respond? Technically nothing, but in

---

[3]Hebrew *Bether* mountains, a location otherwise unknown.

the woman's mind her lover is responding, answering her insistent unspoken desire for his presence. Answering her deepest need, he says, "*Arise, my companion, my fair one, and come!*" He asks that she leave her home, where she seems to be in hiding, and come with him into the country. How can she refuse such an offer? For *lo, the winter* is *past*, the season of winter *rain* is *over and gone*. Spring with its new life fills the land, inviting them to share the renewed joy bursting forth around them: *the blossoms appeared in the earth, the time of singing* of the birds has *arrived, the voice of the turtledove* is *heard in* their *land, the fig tree* has *ripened its fruit, and the vines in blossom* have *spread their fragrance*. Every one of their senses—sight (the blossoms); hearing (the singing of birds, including the voice of the turtledove); taste (the ripened fruit); and smell (the fragrance of the blossoms)—insists that they leave together and walk through the renewed paradise of spring. With a heart filled with desire, he pleads with his *companion*, his *fair one*, to *arise* and *come* with him. The whole world belongs to them—thus he speaks of the earth around them not as "the" land, but as "our" land.[4] Still she hides within her house, inaccessible as *doves in the clefts of the rock, in the covert of the cliff*. Let her come forth to him! Let him *see* her body, her *form*, and *hear* her *voice* as she emerges from hiding! For her *voice* is *sweet* and *her form lovely*.

The meaning of the next verse is much disputed, along with the question of who is speaking. Does the woman here answer her lover, or does the woman continue her quotation of the lover's words? The woman's words in v. 16—*My beloved is mine and I am his*—read much more naturally as the beginning of her emotional response to the extended plea of her lover, and not as the second line of a response about catching foxes. I therefore suggest rather that in v. 15 the lover is playfully inviting his beloved to leave her home and join him in a game of catching little foxes in the vineyard. Interpretations

[4]As opposed to interpreters such as Goulder, who understand the unusual possessive phrase "our land" as an indication that the man speaks to a foreigner, and that his lover is a non-Israelite. See Gledhill's *The Message of the Song of Songs* (Downers Grove, IL: InterVarsity Press, 1994), 133.

that understand it this verse as an exhortation to avoid the threat of lascivious boys (the foxes) freight the words with too much seriousness. It is better to understand the words *catch the foxes for us, the little foxes that are ruining the vineyards* as part of the lover's attempt to coax his beloved out into the field with him, away from her family—an ancient equivalent of "come out, come out, wherever you are!" The job of catching foxes provides an excuse for her to come out with him into the vineyards. He has no intention of spending their time actually catching foxes once they are together—as she knows only too well.

The man succeeds in his attempt. His beloved responds, "My beloved is mine and I am his," adding that *he pastures among the lilies*—a reference, in that pastoral spring setting, to his desirability, recalling their time together in the privacy of their forest bed. He is a shepherd who grazes his flock among the lilies, and may be found in that idyllic setting (thus also 4.5, 6.2). Objections that a shepherd would not pasture his flock among lilies miss the point of the poetry. The woman ends with a double entendre and an invitation for him to stay until the time *when the day breathes and the shadows flee*, i.e., until the dawn arrives, *and be like a gazelle and young stag* upon her *cleft mountains* (her breasts). Let him *turn* and go home over the mountains only after he has spent the night with her (the word *turn* is used in the sense of "turning back" in 1 Samuel 22.17; the Septuagint renders it ἀπόστρεψον [*apostrepson*]). That is, not only will she emerge from her house to be with him, but she also invites him to stay with her until the morning.

Reflection: The God Who Pursues

In this passage we see the man visiting his beloved, coming from afar and drawing ever nearer, until he finally stops at her home, *looking through the windows* and *peeking through the lattice*, straining for a look at her. In this image we see our Lord who pursues us. He does this not only by seeking us at the first when we were lost sheep, bringing us home to the safety of his sheepfold after he has found us (Lk 15.4–5), but continues to pursue us throughout our lives, never ceasing to yearn for us even when we fall away through selfishness and sin. When we shut him out of our lives through our lukewarm devotion and worldliness, he continues to stand at the door and knock (Rev 3.20).

The image of the lover coming from afar, *leaping over the mountains and bounding over the hills*, speaks of the heavenly Lord bridging the infinite chasm between God and his lost creation: he comes near us in the incarnation from the far distance of heaven. Looking down upon the children of men who were wandering like lost sheep, he could not endure to behold them oppressed by the devil, and so he came and saved us.[5] Even afterward, when the lost sheep have been reclaimed, he continues his solicitous care and pursues us when we stray again in sin, calling us back to repentance. He who first pursued the entirety of the human race by becoming incarnate also pursues each of his children throughout their life to keep them in his saving fold.

Thus the image of lover seeking his beloved as she lies innocently behind her walls, hidden deep within her house, offers us hope whenever we lie far away from him, hidden deep within our sin. As the lover is not content until he finds his beloved, so Christ will not rest until his love reclaims us, until we emerge from our stubbornness to return to him. Through the prophet Jeremiah, God declared to Israel that he continually sought their repentance, "rising up early and speaking, but you did not hear, and I called you but you did not answer" (Jer 7.13). Christ continues to rise up early and speak to us whenever we stray from him, calling us home with the relentless voice of love. The lover in the Song cannot wait to find his beloved, and so he calls to her as he draws near, allowing her even from a distance to hear *the voice of* her *beloved*. When we stray Christ calls us also, sparing no effort to reclaim us even if he must leap over the

---

[5]From the prayer for the blessing of water in the Orthodox service of holy baptism.

mountains of our stony indifference and bound over the hills of our heartlessness. We hear the voice of our beloved in Scripture, in our conscience, and in the silent hours of the night when we lie awake.

When he finds us and we return to him it becomes spring, a time for joy and new life. Whatever coldness might have afflicted our hearts before, the *winter is past* when Christ draws near, and the hard *rain* which beat down upon us *is over and gone. Blossoms* and beauty finally *appear in the earth* and *the time of singing has arrived.* All around us is joy and lightness of heart. We stand beside our beloved and listen to the singing: "Blessed is the kingdom of the Father and of the Son and of the Holy Spirit!" It is the voice of the turtledove, the utterance of the Holy Spirit. It is heard in the land of the living (Ps 27.13), and in our penitent heart.

5

The Woman seeks her lover by night (3.1–5)

The Woman:

₃.₁On my bed nightly
I sought my soul's beloved;
I sought him but did not find him.
₂I will arise now and go about the city;
in the streets and in the squares
I will seek my soul's beloved.
I sought him but did not find him.
₃The watchmen found me, who make the rounds
    in the city,
and I said, "My soul's beloved—have you seen
    him?"
₄Scarcely had I left them
when I found my soul's beloved;
I held on to him and would not let him go
until I had brought him to my mother's house,
and into the chamber of her who conceived me.
₅I adjure you, O daughters of Jerusalem,
by the gazelles or by the does of the field,
that you will not arouse or awaken the love
until he pleases.

The poetry we find in 2.8–17, where the woman is hidden from him in her home just as doves remain hidden in the clefts of the rock, is balanced by the poetry of 3.1–5, where the woman searches for him.

The balance is complete: he first searches for her in the daytime and finds her hidden in her home, calling her into the country; she then searches for him in the nighttime, leaving her home to seek him in the streets of the city. Common to both poems is the desire of each for the other—a desire that compels them to undertake a search and which ends in the satisfaction of their desire. These poetic lines thus express the timeless longing of the lover for the beloved, a longing that grows fonder in periods of absence and separation. Because the lovers are one flesh (Gen 2.24; cf. Mt 19.5; 1 Cor 6.16) their separation is felt keenly, and it pushes each to seek out the beloved.

This scene opens with the woman *on* her *bed, nightly seeking* her *soul's beloved*. For her the pain of separation is not a one-time experience; it constantly attends those occasions when they are apart, especially when she is on her bed alone, without his desired presence beside her. The Hebrew text states that she sought him "in the nights" (plural)—night after night, in other words, and not simply on one occasion. This seeking is an interior emotional search as she lies on her bed. She does not actually look all around the bedroom to see if he is there, for she knows he is not, but still she looks for his presence in her heart. The intensity of her desire is expressed in her title for him: he is not simply "my" beloved but "my soul's" beloved (a phrase repeated four times in three verses), the love of her life, the treasure of her very existence. Though absent from the more reliable Hebrew manuscripts, the Septuagint adds a line in which she calls out his name in the night: "I called him, but he did not answer me." This captures the spirit of her reminiscence: from her bed, night after night, she desires him so much that she calls out his name.

Eventually she can stand his absence no longer. She makes a decision requiring a perhaps foolhardy courage: she will arise, leave her home, and search for him in the city in the middle of the night. Protestations that women were unlikely to do this in that culture are beside the point, since this is poetry, not a memoir; one could include such an action in a poem even if one would not actually do it in real life. Her determination is expressed in the line "I will arise now."[1] It is the decision of someone overcoming fear, intent on the moment of reunion, desire trampling down discretion. She recounts the futility of her search simply: "I sought him, but did not find him." Behind these words stands the experience of her cold and vain striding through streets, fruitlessly peering around corners as each failure weighs upon her heart. But though she did not find him, *the watchmen who make rounds in the city* find her. In response to their inquiries as to what she is doing, wandering alone about the *streets* and open *squares* of the city, i.e., throughout the entire city, both the narrow lanes and the wide spaces, she asks her own question: "My soul's beloved—have you seen him?" This repeated inquiry shows the depth of her desire, for it reveals that she is not concerned about justifying herself, nor even giving thought to her own safety, but entirely fixated upon her lover.

Then comes the joyful moment she has hoped for. *Scarcely had she left them when* she *found* her *soul's beloved.* The intensity of the moment of her determined desire shines through her brief description of the time of discovery: *I held on to him and would not let him go until I had brought him to my mother's house.* She does not relate what she says to him at the instant of discovery nor his reply, for she does not need to. The tenacity of her grasp and her clinging to him as she steers him to her home says it all. Her room is now described further as *the chamber of her who conceived me.* That is, she defines the room as the place of sexual union where she herself was first conceived, and it takes little imagination to see why and what would transpire there next. Once again, a curtain of poetic delicacy is drawn over their intimacy. The adjuration of 2.7 is repeated, and for the same reason. Again, no doubt, his *left hand* will *be under* her *head* and his *right hand* will *embrace her* (2.6). Like the search and encounter of 2.8–17, this search also ends in discovery and joy.

---

[1] The utterance of the Prodigal Son upon coming to repentance (Lk 15.18).

Reflection: The Pain of Absence

In this section the woman pines after her lover, missing him through the long nights. Eventually, when she can stand his absence no longer, she leaves the safety of her room to seek him along the streets and open squares. Her continued fruitless inquiries testify to the length of her search and her determination to find him at all costs. Suddenly she does find him, and the couple is joyfully reunited in the privacy of her mother's bedroom.

This brief story expresses the pain of soul that every believer experiences during times of spiritual dryness. The believer remembers poignantly the times of the sweet presence of God: "These things I remember, and I pour out my soul within me. For I used to go along with the throng and lead them in procession to the house of God, with the voice of joy and thanksgiving, a multitude keeping festival" (Ps 42.4). Now all is arid and empty; the former closeness to God has departed. The soul is in despair, disturbed within (Ps 42.5).

The woman *on her bed nightly sought* her *soul's beloved, but did not find him*. The breakers and waves of despair roll over her, but despite this she continues to cling to the hope of reunion. The memory of their sweet time together remains with her in the night like a song, a prayer to the God of her life (Ps 42.7–8).

The time of spiritual dryness, which is characterized by the apparent departure of Christ, does not last forever. If we continue to seek the Lord, refusing to give up and persevering with the same determination that the woman showed when she arose and went about the city's streets and squares, we will eventually find the Lord. Amidst the pain of absence it is important to remember what we have lost: not a mere experience, but our *soul's beloved*, the One who is everything to us and without whom life holds neither joy nor value. The woman's repeated inquiries to the *watchmen* who *make the rounds in the city* encourage us to seek the Lord, pouring out our prayer again and again and imploring his presence. The woman's testimony that "scarcely had I left them [the watchmen] when I found my soul's beloved" assures us that we too shall find the Lord, and the time of dryness and aridity will come to an end. Just as she comes upon her beloved suddenly, unexpectedly, the Lord will quickly return to the soul that perseveres in seeking him.

The woman's further testimony (*I held on to him and would not let him go*) reveals the intensity of her joy and her fulfilled desire. We can see her clinging to him in a frenzy of joy, hardly daring to let go lest she lose him again. This expresses the spiritual reunion of the soul with her Lord and the sweetness of restored worship. Mary Magdalene was forbidden by her Lord to cling to him after she first found him after his resurrection, for as he said, "I have not yet ascended to the Father" (Jn 20.17). The implication is that she may cling to him later, in the Spirit, after he *has* ascended to the Father.

It is this spiritual embrace that is prophetically imaged here. We may gauge the depth of this embrace by the fact that it finds consummation when she *brought him to* her *mother's house*—a clear reference to sexual union, since this house is further described as *the chamber of her who conceived me*. Their intimate union finds its parallel fulfillment in our spiritual union with Christ. Paul refers to man and woman, who are joined together to become one flesh, as an example of the believer and the Lord who become "one spirit" together (1 Cor 6.16–17). We are spiritually joined to the Lord as one spirit with him, clinging to him in love, refusing to let him go. The pain of spiritual absence will not endure forever; weeping may last one night, but joy, as Mary Magdalene discovered, comes in the morning (Ps 30.5).

6

The marriage of King Solomon
(3.6–11)

The Woman:

3.6What is this coming up from the wilderness
like columns of smoke,
perfumed with myrrh and frankincense,
with all kinds of powders of the merchant?
7Behold, it is the litter of Solomon!
Sixty warriors surround it,
of the warriors of Israel.
8All of them skilled with the sword,
trained in war;
each man has his sword at his side,
against the terrors of the night.
9King Solomon has made a sedan chair for himself,
from the wood of Lebanon.
10He made its posts of silver,
its canopy of gold,
and its seat of purple fabric,
with its interior woven with love
by the daughters of Jerusalem.
11Go forth, O daughters of Zion,
and gaze on King Solomon with the crown
with which his mother has crowned him
on the day of his wedding,
and on the day of his gladness of heart.

The scene shifts once again as we are offered a new facet of the woman's delight in her lover. When the poetic curtain lifts, we see something *coming up from the wilderness*, emerging gradually from the backdrop of the distant horizon. "What is this?" the woman asks. All she can see from a distance are *columns of smoke*, the dust clouds kicked up by the awe-inspiring retinue mingling with the clouds of incense from the burning of *myrrh and frankincense and all kinds of powders of the merchant*, for such variety could only be purchased from afar. Eventually it comes closer, and she can see *it is the litter of Solomon*. Her surprise and delight are signaled by an initial cry of *behold*. It is impressive indeed, as befits Israel's mighty king: *sixty warriors surround it*, true *warriors of Israel, all of them skilled with the sword, trained in war*. Their great number—King David mentioned only thirty mighty men in 2 Samuel 23.18f—and elite expertise mark them as worthy of such a king. They function as his guard of honor, and their imposing presence and the daunting *swords* at their *sides* (making them well able to defend the king from night ambush and *the terrors of the night*) add to the glory of the procession.

At length *King Solomon* himself comes into view, seated upon the stately *sedan chair* that he *had made for himself*. This glorious palanquin, made from the best *wood*, the timber *of Lebanon*, has *posts of silver* propping up a *canopy of gold* and a *seat of purple fabric*. Enhancing the glory of the king on this day is the love of his people, for the *interior* of the sedan chair had been *woven with love by the daughters of Jerusalem*.

The day itself is a national celebration. This aspect of the king's glory and upcoming nuptials finds expression in the characterization of the women of Jerusalem as *daughters of Zion*. This wording, along with the description of the attendants as *warriors of Israel*, expresses the glory of the day. The words *Israel* and *Zion*, which set events upon a national stage that goes beyond the personal love of the couple, are found nowhere else in the Song. If up until now the Song has celebrated a private love, we now see that this love is something to be celebrated by the entire nation. No wonder the woman tells the other women of Jerusalem to *go forth and gaze on King Solomon* on the *day of his wedding*. He wears a nuptial *crown*[1] (this would be a special adornment for his wedding, not the crown worn at his coronation), the one *with which his mother crowned him.* Mention of King Solomon's *mother*—she remains nameless since this is poetry, not biography—conveys the delight of his entire family in his upcoming wedding. His bride is no unwelcome intruder; rather, she is a cause for rejoicing among those who know and love the King and share *his gladness of heart.*

We may well wonder how these lines of poetry fit into the total poem. The tone here is very different from the rest of the Song, which focuses on an intimate dialogue between the man and his beloved. Indeed, some interpreters[2] deny that the woman is present in these lines at all, assigning them to the chorus.[3] Certainly these verses contain no eroticism. What is their purpose?

Here the Song focuses upon the glamor of the relationship between the girl and the king. The inequality of social standing between royalty and commoner contributes to the latter's attractiveness as a Cinderella figure. Her low status is hinted at in 1.5–6, in which she admits that she was forced to work in the fields. The king's glamor as a royal figure of power and wealth is also suggested in 1.5 (the exquisite curtains of Solomon) as well as in 1.4 and 1.12 (the king's royal chambers and his couch). Now these hints at high royal status come to the fore, and we glimpse the excitement that the woman feels knowing that her lover is the mighty king of Israel

[1]A glorious enough sight to serve as an image for national restoration in Isaiah 61.10, and a reminder to an Orthodox priest or deacon of his high calling, since he recites the verse while putting on his sticharion before the liturgy.

[2]Garrett, *Song of Songs*, 175f.

[3]This interpretation makes the woman the one who draws near in the sedan chair. But this contradicts 3.7, which identifies it as the sedan chair of Solomon. It is possible that the author means that it is the woman who sits in Solomon's own sedan chair, but this reading is counterintuitive given the directive for the daughters of Jerusalem to go forth and look at Solomon (3.11). If she is the one who draws near in the sedan chair, it seems odd that she would be completely ignored while Solomon himself is described in v. 11.

(note that the name Solomon is mentioned three times within five verses). Despite her lowly origins, her lover is the nation's leader. The wealth she beholds in his retinue and royal palanquin as they draw near is part of his attractiveness and allure. She can hardly believe her good fortune in finding him. This sense of wonder will find further expression in 6.12, where she declares that she can hardly recognize herself now that she has been swept up to share the royal chariot with her beloved.

Reflection: The Glory of the King

As noted above, this passage is unlike the rest of the Song, for the woman's other utterances, whether addressed to her lover or about him, e.g., 1.16, 5.10f, contain words of tender endearment. They presuppose intimate familiarity and delight in close private proximity. But now the king is seen from afar, rather than in his intimate chamber (as in 1.4, 12). We find neither terms of endearment nor erotic familiarity. She is entranced by his public grandeur and impressive royal persona, not by his whispered words of love. Instead of his couch, he is on his royal palanquin; not alone with her but surrounded by his fearsome royal bodyguard of sixty armed warriors. Having exulted in his private charms, she now exults in his public glory. This passage is all about the glamor that attends being the beloved of a mighty king.

When transposed into the spiritual setting of the soul's love for her Lord, we see an expression of the balance necessary for a healthy spiritual life. Christ the lover of our souls, the intimate bridegroom of the Church, is also the exalted Lord who rules over heaven and earth. He is borne on the throne of the cherubim, the Lord of the seraphim and King of Israel: he alone is holy and rests among his holy ones.[4] St John the beloved disciple may have leaned upon his master's breast at the Last Supper (Jn 13.23), but he also fell at his feet as one dead when he beheld his ascended glory (Rev 1.17).

[4]From the prayer that the celebrant priest says privately, just prior to the great entrance of the Orthodox Divine Liturgy.

A proper relationship with Christ combines these two postures, for we know Christ both as intimate friend and exalted Lord. Christ is closer to us than our own breath, and yet at the same time entirely separated from sinners and exalted above the heavens (Heb 7.26). The latter is required if the former is not to degenerate into a casual emotionalism, devoid of proper reverence. The former is required if the latter is not to morph into the worship of another unknown god, one too distant for us to love.

The woman sees the king coming from a distance, *up from the wilderness*. At first she cannot see him, only *columns of smoke*, a dust cloud kicked up by his retinue combining with clouds of *myrrh and frankincense*. Only gradually does he come into view, allowing her to recognize *the litter of* her beloved *Solomon* surrounded by *sixty warriors*. The picture of the king approaching from a great distance with his armed retinue is a picture of Christ, who is exalted above the heavens and surrounded by his holy angels and all the court of heaven. The woman focuses upon two details: the king's *sedan chair woven with love by the daughters of Jerusalem*, and the *crown* placed upon his head by *his mother*. The reference to these women shows how beloved the King is by the residents of his city, and prophetically reveals that Christ is loved and praised by all—those in the heavenly Jerusalem along with those on earth below. Mention of the king's chair and crown serve to accent his royal authority.

The picture is necessary for us who draw near to the Lord and experience his closeness as we eat his flesh and drink his blood during the Divine Liturgy. Though the priests hold him in their hands, and though all the communing faithful consume him with their mouths, he yet remains the King of glory, ever eaten and, yet never consumed, sanctifying all those who partake of him.[5] Only by remembering how exalted is our ascended Lord can we truly and fruitfully have intimate communion of prayer with him and savingly draw near to him in the fear of God and with faith.

---

[5]These words are said at the division of the Lamb at the Divine Liturgy.

7

The Man woos his beloved (4.1–5.1)

The Man:

4.1Behold, you are fair, my companion,
behold, you are fair!
Your eyes are doves behind your veil;
your hair like a flock of goats
descending Mount Gilead.
2Your teeth are like a shorn flock
that has come up from the wash,
all of which bear twins,
and not one among them has lost her young.
3Your lips are like a scarlet thread,
and your mouth is lovely.
Your cheeks are like slices of pomegranate,
behind your veil.
4Your neck is like the tower of David,
built in layers
on which are hung a thousand shields,
all the armor of the warriors.
5Your two breasts are like two fawns,
twins of a gazelle
which pasture among the lilies.
6When the day breathes
and the shadows flee,
I will go my way to the mountain of myrrh

and to the hill of frankincense.
₇You are altogether fair, my companion,
and there is no blemish in you.

A new dialogue of intimacy opens between the man and his beloved. He discovers her beauty afresh, prefacing the declaration of praise *you are fair* with *behold*, as if each time he looks upon her he cannot believe what he is seeing. Like one admiring a work of art, his eyes lovingly linger upon each feature as she stands still before his ravished gaze. He begins quite naturally with her eyes, since they have obviously been staring at each other: her *eyes were like doves behind her veil.* Unlike the reference to doves in 1.15, here in 4.1 and again in 4.3 we find mention of a *veil*, in this case probably a diaphanous veil, since both her eyes and her cheeks can be seen behind it. Given the reference to breasts in 4.5, we may perhaps conclude that the man is not simply admiring his beloved but also undressing her, for by the time he praises her attributes in v. 5 her veil has clearly been removed.

Admiring her beauty, he then likens her *hair* to *a flock of goats.* When one sees *a flock of goats* (usually black in color) *descending* a steep a trail such as those found on *Mount Gilead*, they look like a black flowing stream. Her long flowing hair reminds him of this beautiful sight. These black tresses contrast with her white teeth and red lips, both of which are seen as she smiles for him. Her *teeth* are white as a *shorn flock* of sheep that has just *come up from the wash*, white, clean and sparkling. Furthermore, *all of* [these sheep] *bear twins and not one among them has lost her young.* Here the imagery evokes a ewe with her two baby lambs trailing behind. As each ewe has two lambs, so too the women's smile reveals a complete set of teeth, each one above finding its match with a tooth below. A full set of teeth is taken for granted today thanks to good dentistry, but it was otherwise in ancient times when teeth were often yellowed and missing. Not so with this woman—her radiant smile reveals a full set of even, white teeth. Her *lips*, drawn back in a smile, resemble *a scarlet thread*, a *mouth* which is truly *lovely*. And her *cheeks* are *like slices of pomegranate behind* her *veil*—that is, a gentle rosy color.

Working his way down, he admires her *neck*, which reminds him of *the tower of David*. This tower may be an allusion to any tower in the city of David, but it cannot be identified with the main structure in Jerusalem at that name, for it dates only from the time of King Herod. Perhaps the *tower of David* indicates that her neck is as regal and strong as David was, but it is equally possible that he specifies a *tower* because it had many *shields* hung upon it ("a thousand" is typical Oriental hyperbole). It was not uncommon for shields to adorn towers; thus, for example, we read in Ezekiel 27.11, "The sons of Arvad and your army were on your walls and the brave men were in your towers. They hung their shields on your walls; they perfected your beauty." The sight of her regal neck, adorned with many overlapping necklaces, reminds him of the sight of that tower decked with such *armor*.

In his descending survey of her beautiful form he comes next to her two breasts, which he compares to *two fawns, twins of a gazelle*. That is, they are graceful, sprightly, beautiful, perfectly paired. The fawns are described as *pasturing among the lilies*. The phrase also appears in 2.16, where the woman describes her lover as "pasturing among the lilies." This tells us that the image here is not meant to be visual but emotional. A flock of fawns grazing among a field of lilies bears no physical resemblance to her breasts, but the beauty of that scene moved him then, just as the beauty of her breasts moves him now. The lilies also recall their idyllic forest trysts together.

The totality of her beauty inspires him to stay and spend all night making love. He will stay until the time *when the day breathes and the shadows flee* (daybreak), spending his time on *the mountain of myrrh and the hill of frankincense*. Like the reference in 2.16 to "the mountains of Bether," these summits are not geographical places within Palestine. Rather, they are references to her perfumed breasts—that is the destination to which he will *go his way*. He ends his description of her beauty by saying that she is *altogether fair*: from head to toe there is *no blemish* in her. She is perfection itself.

> *The Man*:
>
> ₄.₈Come with me from Lebanon, O bride,
> with me from Lebanon!
> Travel from the top of Amana,
> from the top of Senir and Hermon,
> from the dens of lions,
> from the lairs of leopards.
> ₉You have captured my heart, my sister bride;
> you have ravished my heart with one glance of your
>   eyes,
> with one strand of your necklace.

The man goes on to entreat his beloved to *come with* him *from Lebanon*, to *travel from the top of Amana, Senir, and Hermon, from the dens of lions and the lairs of leopards*. The references to Amana, Senir, and Hermon are to mountains north of Palestine, in the region of *Lebanon*. According to Deuteronomy 3.9, Senir is the old Amorite name for Hermon, whereas 1 Chronicles 5.23 seems to distinguish between Senir and Hermon. (Evidently there was some fluidity of usage between the time these two books were written.) The precise geographical details, however, are less important than their general location: in the far north, a place not only distant but dangerous, for it contains *the dens of lions*, and *the lairs of leopards* who dwelt in that mountainous region.

Why, however, does man entreat her to leave such a distant place to come with him? Does she actually live in the far north? It seems clear that the man is situating his beloved in that region emotionally, not geographically. Her demeanor is aloof, distant, her heart apparently far away. It is the kind of thing we might say today to someone who seems distant and distracted: "Where are you?" We know where the person is physically; our question concerns the emotional state. And so it is here: she is not warm to him, not responsive. Drawing near to her in intimacy seems to be fraught with danger and difficulty, like scaling the summits of high distant mountains populated with wild animals. Let her *travel* down from such cold and unattainable heights and *come with* him! It is an invitation to greater warmth and responsiveness, greater intimacy.

We may ask why the woman, formerly so ardent, now seems cold to her lover. I suggest that her apparent indifference is part of the game of love. Formerly the man invited the woman to chase him (1.8); now, by her unresponsiveness, she is inviting him to chase her. She is not actually indifferent, but pretends to be cold and distant to stir him to greater fervor. As we can see, her loving stratagem works for her. A quick look at the history of men and women reveals that it has worked for other women as well. The Song thus offers us a glimpse into the timeless and beautiful games that lovers in every generation delight to play.

When entreating his lover he calls her his *bride* (1.8, 11) and even *sister bride* (9, 10). This latter term of affection sounds rather odd today. The term of endearment "my bride" is clear enough, for it refers to his sexual attachment to her as his spouse. The term "sister," however, seems more problematic. Again, the reference is to his emotional attachment—he uses this term to express an emotional closeness to her, such as he feels toward his own sister, his own flesh and blood. The combined "my sister bride" is his declaration that he feels completely joined to her, body and soul.

Not only does he feel completely one with her in every way, he declares that she *has captured* his *heart*. The word *ravished* has been variously rendered, with some translations opting for "captured," "stolen," or "wounded." The Septuagint says "you heartened us." Whatever the verb chosen, it is clear that the woman has a serious effect on him, for the heart was considered the seat of thought and will and not merely that of emotion, as we believe today. By saying, "You have ravished my heart," the man confesses that he cannot function without her, and that all his powers are in her hand. Such is her power that he is undone by *one glance of* her *eye, one strand of* her *necklace.* She has already confessed that he has conquered her (2.4, *his banner over me is love*), but he now confesses the same: *she* has conquered *him*—and with complete ease. A single look from her is all it took, a mere glimpse of one of her necklace strands. No wonder he pleads with her to descend from the cold summits of Amana, Senir, and Hermon!

> *The Man*:
>
> 4.10How fair are your caresses, my sister bride!
> How much better are your caresses than wine,
> and the fragrance of your anointing oils
> than all kinds of spices!
> 11Your lips, O bride, drip liquid honey;
> honey and milk are under your tongue,
> and the fragrance of your garments is like the
>   fragrance of Lebanon.
> 12A garden locked is my sister bride,
> A garden locked, a fountain sealed.
> 13Your shoots are an orchard of pomegranates
> with choice fruits, henna blossoms and nard plants,
> 14nard and saffron, calamus and cinnamon,
> with all the trees of frankincense,
> myrrh and aloes, with all the chief spices.
> 15You are a garden fountain,
> a well of fresh water,
> flowing from Lebanon.

The man continues to praise his beloved, once again calling her his *sister bride* (5.10, 12). Her *caresses* are *fair*—indeed, he repeats, her *caresses* are *better* and more intoxicating *than wine*. As he draws near to kiss her and be caressed, *the fragrance of* her *anointing-oils* and perfumes are richer and more heady than *all kinds of spices.* So enamored is he with her kisses and scent that he repeats his praise again: the *lips* of his bride *drip liquid honey*—indeed, both *honey and milk are under* her *tongue,* and *the fragrance of* her *garments* is like the luxurious *fragrance of* exotic *Lebanon.* He cannot pull his mind away from her kisses or her fragrance, for both linger in his taste and smell.

The reference to *honey and milk* as well as *liquid honey,* i.e., honey dripping from the honeycomb, refer to how sweet her kisses are. It is possible that the line about her lips dripping honey refers to her sweet *words* (as Proverbs 5.3 describes the lips of an adulteress dripping honey), but given the concentration here on her caresses (4.10), the words more probably refer to kisses.

The combination of honey and milk is also a traditional image of luxury, and the classic description of the promised land (Ex 3.8, 33.3, Num 13.27). The woman's kisses are therefore the height of luxury and lavish sweetness. The potency of the image is lost in our culture, where we enjoy a constant supply of sugar. The ancients, who had a constant sweet tooth, but no constant supply of sweets, valued honey very highly because of its scarcity. Honey for the ancients offered an almost dreamy euphoria—as do the kisses from the man's beloved.

The man delights in their exclusive love: she is *a garden locked, a fountain sealed. Garden* (Hebrew *gan*) does not mean not a little patch of vegetables or flowers, but a park or orchard that in this case is *locked* (enclosed by a wall or a hedge with a bolted gate). A *fountain* that has been *sealed* is one similarly protected for its rightful owner. The metaphor here does not refer to the woman's virginity, since the description forms part of a long declaration of how sweet her sexual favors were. Rather, the metaphor refers to the mutual exclusivity of their love—no one can enter that garden or drink from that fountain except him. Earlier she says, "My beloved is mine and I am his" (2.16), declaring that they belong only to each other. Here her beloved says the same, acknowledging that she does indeed belong to him alone.

The man continues the metaphor of his beloved as a garden, in this case an orchard. The word rendered here as *orchard* is the Hebrew *pardes*, an Old Persian loan word from which the word "paradise" is derived. His description is indeed one of paradise. Indeed, it is doubtful that all these plants could have been found in one Palestinian orchard. We have instead a fantasy garden, containing all that is pleasant and pleasing in a single paradisal place.

Her *shoots* (an elaborate metaphor involving plants) refer to the delights her lovemaking offers him. He compares these shoots to an orchard which includes *pomegranates* (a classic love fruit); *choice fruits* such as *henna and nard plants* (cultivated for their pleasing blossoms and fragrance); *saffron, calamus* (or cane), both of which have oils which give forth a strong scent; *cinnamon* with its aromatic bark; and *frankincense, myrrh,* and *aloes*, all of which were used to perfume the garments of the wealthy (cf. Ps 45.8). The orchard is one to overwhelm the senses, and these *chief spices* are his beloved's *shoots*—a reference to her loving caresses and her lovemaking. She is indeed a *garden* for him and a *fountain*, a source of pleasure and life. In a dry and arid land, she is his *well of fresh water, flowing from Lebanon*, fresh and cold as water flowing from the mountain snow. In a weary world, she is his source of refreshment and vigor.

Reflection: The King Praises His Beloved

In this long section the man praises his beloved in some detail, beginning at the top and working his delighted way down. Ancient exegetes worked hard to find significance in each of the anatomical details. One commentator viewed the two breasts of the woman as "the two sons of Aaron, Eleazar and Phineas, who were the first to serve under the Law that regulated the priesthood," with the chest from which the breasts grew understood as Aaron himself, since the function of priests, then as now, was to "present to their hearers the milk of their doctrine."[1] St Gregory of Nyssa, reading from

[1]Richard A. Norris, Jr., trans. and ed., *The Song of Songs: Interpreted by Early Christian and Medieval Commentators* (Grand Rapids: William B. Eerdmans Pub-

his Septuagint that the bride had heartened her bridegroom "with one of your eyes" (instead of *one glance of your eyes*) constructs an elaborate explanation wherein

> the soul's work of seeing is twofold: there is one operation by which it sees the truth, and another that is led astray by attending to things that amount to nothing. And since the Bride's pure eye is open only to the nature of the good, while the other is inactive, the friends for this reason give praise to *one* of her eyes, by whose sole means she contemplates the only One [God].[2]

Our own allegorical approach avoids freighting the individual metaphors with specific significance. In this extended passage the king praises his beloved for her beauty, professing himself entirely smitten with her. That is, the passage is about the woman's beauty and the king's love for her, and it is this general message that we may transpose into a spiritual setting. Regarding this love of Christ for his Church, we may say four things.

First, the beauty of the bride provides an image of the beauty of Christ's bride, the Church, and of individual believing souls within her. Though our liturgical tradition focuses upon the believer's unworthiness and sin as way of inculcating humility—for example, in the eucharistic prayer of access we confess that Christ came into the world to save sinners "of whom I am first" (1 Tim 1.15)—we find a complementary truth in the Scriptures. That is, we find an assertion of the holiness of the believer, an assertion that the Christian is different from those outside the church.

Thus St Paul consistently refers to the Christians as "saints" (1 Cor 1.2; Eph 5.3; Col 1.2), describing them as "blameless and innocent, children of God above reproach in the midst of a crooked and perverse generation, among whom [they] shone as lights in the world" (Phil 2.15). If they persevere in the faith, they might be

lishing Company, 2003), 165 [quoting Apponius, a fourth- to seventh-century Latin writer known only from his commentary on the Song of Songs.—*Ed.*].

[2]Gregory of Nyssa, *Homily* 1 (*GNO* 6:257–58). Translation in *Homilies*, 271.

presented "holy and blameless and beyond reproach" (Col 1.22). The one who abides in Christ does not sin (1 Jn 3.6), and if those who keep the faith do not stumble in apostasy, they will "stand in the presence of his glory blameless with great joy" (Jude 24). They will walk with Christ "in white, for they are worthy" (Rev 3.4). Such references to the believer's worthiness do not mean, of course, that we are saved by works apart from God's forgiveness and grace. These references do not describe the state of the believer in comparison to God, but only when compared to the state of the world. The true believer hates sin and strives after righteousness in penitent lowliness, thus remaining a stranger to the world's rebellion against God.

This is the very beauty that the king prizes and praises in his bride. Christ looks upon his bride and declares, "You are altogether fair, my companion, and there is no blemish in you" (Song 4.7). At the last day he will present his bride as one "glorious, having no spot or wrinkle or any such thing"; she will be "holy and blameless" (Eph 5.27). We will come to that final wedding banquet in beauty, for "it was given to [the bride] to clothe herself in fine linen, bright and clean, for the fine linen is the righteous acts of the saints" (Rev 19.8). It is these righteous acts that constitute our adornment and preparation to meet our Husband (Rev 21.2). We resist being seduced by the serpent so that we may retain our inner beauty and be presented to Christ as a pure virgin (2 Cor 11.2–3).

Secondly, we see in this passage the burning love of the king for his beloved. He declares that she has *captured* his *heart*—indeed, *ravished* his *heart with* but *one glance of* her *eyes* (4.9). Here we see the overwhelming love that Christ has for his creation, and for his bride. We too easily imagine God impassibly sitting on his heavenly throne, untouched by our rejection of him. While theology indeed affirms God's impassibility, this does not mean that he remains aloof. Both the Old Testament and the New repeatedly affirm that God is broken-hearted over the sins and rejection of his children. Thus God's song in Isaiah 5.1 f, proclaiming that despite all the care God has lavished on his vineyard, it produced no good grapes, only worthless wild grapes. And thus also Micah 6.3f, wherein God brings a lawsuit before his people, asking the mountains and hills to function as witnesses: "My people, what have I done to you, and how have I wearied you? Answer me! Indeed, I brought you up from the land of Egypt and ransomed you from the house of slavery." One can almost feel in these passages the divine heartbreak and perplexity at Israel's perverse rejection of his love. Or consider our Lord's lament over Jerusalem: "O Jerusalem, Jerusalem, who kills the prophets and stones those who are sent to her! How often I wanted to gather your children together, the way a hen gathers her chicks under her wings, and you were unwilling" (Mt 23.37). Taken together, these passages witness to God's heartbreak over his rejection by those whom he loves. The intensity of the heartbreak reveals also the immensity of his love.

Thirdly, we note here the unusual term of endearment wherein the king repeatedly refers to his beloved as his "sister bride" (4.8, 9, 10, 12). In our exegesis we indicated that this term refers to the bond that the man feels for his beloved, declaring that along with the sexual closeness of a man with his bride, he also feels the domestic emotional closeness of a man for his sister. When transposed into a spiritual setting, the term expresses the two natures of Christ: his consubstantiality with our nature, and his divine consubstantiality with the Father.

With regard to Christ's human nature, we are indeed his *sister*, for the term witnesses to his likeness with us and the fact that we share the same Father. Thus Hebrews 2.11: "Both he who sanctifies [i.e., Christ] and those who are sanctified [his Church] are all from one [the Father], for which reason he is not ashamed to call them brethren." In the condescension of his incarnation, Christ assumes an equality with us, the equality of siblings. But regarding his divine nature we are Christ's bride, and he is our bridegroom. As the bridegroom, he is the Savior of the body, the divine Lord and Master to whom his bride submits as to her husband (Eph 5.23–24). Thus the term "bride," when applied to the Church, witnesses to Christ's difference from us and to his superior divine nature. Yet both natures witness to his overwhelming love for us, since out of love he became one of us and took us for his bride.

Fourthly, we note here the exclusivity of our devotion to Jesus: we are *a garden locked, a fountain sealed*, open only to our divine Lover and closed off from all others. In the world we have many godly allegiances—family, tribe, nation—that require loyalty. But these must be subordinated to our loyalty and allegiance to Jesus. If it comes to a choice between even the most binding loyalty to family and loyalty to Jesus, we are prepared instantly to hate our families, that is, to reject their claims on us in order to choose Christ (Lk 14.26). We see this exclusive dedication to Christ in the second prayer for Pentecost vespers: "Against you alone do we sin, but you alone do we also adore. We know not how to worship a strange god, nor how to stretch forth our hands to any other god, O Master." We have been betrothed as a pure virgin to Christ (2 Cor 11.2), and our hearts belong to him alone.

> *The Woman:*
>
> 4.16Awake, north wind,
> and come, wind of the south;
> breathe upon my garden!
> Let its spices flow.
> May my beloved come into his garden
> and eat its choice fruits!

The woman at last responds to her lover's long and passionate entreaties. Although she seemed as cold and distant as the mountains of Lebanon, her desire was always for him. And so she cries out, "*Awake, north wind, and come, wind of south, breathe upon my garden.*" The wind from the north was a cold wind, while the wind from the south was a warm one, but these meteorological details are irrelevant. By invoking by the winds of the *north* and the *south,* the woman opens herself up to all winds, inviting them to *breathe upon* her *garden* and *let its spices* (fragrance) *flow* to her lover. She thereby declares herself completely open to pleasing him.

We should not miss the psychologically brilliant and subtle nuance present here. The man has just finished a long speech, imploring her to come with him. But instead of immediately responding to him directly—"*May my beloved come into his garden and eat its choice fruits*"—her first words are directed to to the north and south winds. By not replying affirmatively and giving in to him at once, she keeps him waiting in suspense just a moment longer, speaking first to the winds. He will have to wait a bit longer, listening to her invitation to the winds before concluding that she is giving in. We see again the woman's brilliance in pretending to be as cold as the mountains of distant Lebanon. She knows how to make him wait, and for just how long.

Her surrender, when it comes, is total. In her invitation to the winds, she asks them to *breathe upon* her *garden*, but in the invitation that immediately follows she describes herself as *his* garden. She is telling her lover that she belongs to him, completely and exclusively. The metaphor of *coming into a garden* and *eating its choice fruits* is of course a metaphor for sexual feasting.

Reflection: Awake North Wind!

In response to her lover's comparing her to a garden, the woman offers him an invitation to *come into* that *garden and* to *eat its choice fruits*. Just before that invitation she invokes the *north wind* and the *south wind*, asking them to *awake* and *breathe* upon the garden, to let *its spices flow* toward her lover. What is the deeper meaning of this invocation? Ancient exegetes tended to view the winds negatively. Based on the Septuagint reading of Proverbs 27.16 ("The north wind is a harsh wind, even though it is called by an auspicious name"),[3] they viewed the north wind as bringing evil. Indeed, the north wind

[3]The Hebrew reads, "He who would restrain her [i.e., the contentious woman of the previous verse] restrains the wind, and grasps oil with his right hand."

brings cold into Palestine, while the south wind brings warmth. Accordingly, some exegetes contrasted the two winds, seeing in the north wind the chill of evil and in the south wind the warmth of goodness.

Not all the ancient exegetes, however, contrasted the north and south winds. The Venerable Bede viewed them similarly, writing, "By north wind or south wind [Solomon] indicates the tempestuous blasts of the repeated temptations by which the Church was to be struck in order that she might learn that the degree of spiritual grace within her would correspond to that of her interior virtue"—in other words, the blasts of the various winds of trial stimulate the Church to bring forth the fragrance of virtue.[4]

Despite such interpretations, the Song seems to make clear that the winds, whether from north or south, are positive. They allow the fragrances of the garden to flow forth, which is why the woman bids the winds to *awake* and *come*. The winds are less a meteorological reference than a merism,[5] intended to denote the totality of winds from every direction and to express the woman's complete openness to her lover. With the help of such winds, she hopes that her loving desire will flow to her lover, drawing him to herself.

Although the Hebrew terms used for "north wind" (*zaphon*) and "south wind" (*teman*) do not contain the word *ruach* (wind), the concept of wind remains nonetheless. We recall many positive references to wind in Scripture. Thus, for example, at the beginning of creation the *ruach* of God hovered over the face of the primordial deep to give life (Gen 1.2); God sent a *ruach* to pass over the earth after Noah's flood (Gen 8.1) and to part the waters of the Red Sea at the exodus (Ex 14.21). Ezekiel was told to call *ruach* from the four winds to give breath and life to the dead in the valley of dry bones (Ezek 37.9). Given this history, it is not surprising that God should send his Spirit upon the disciples on the day of Pentecost as a mighty

[4]Norris, *Song of Songs*, 191–92.

[5]I.e., a rhetorical device that refers to a single thing either by referring to several of its parts or by using more than one synonymn for the single subject in question (here, using the north and south winds to refer to wind in general).—*Ed.*

rushing wind (Acts 2.1–4). Indeed, the Hebrew word *ruach* means wind, breath, and spirit.

If we transpose to a spiritual setting the woman's call to the winds for help in wafting her fragrances towards her lover, we may see in these winds a typological allusion to the Holy Spirit. The bride of Christ indeed possesses spiritual beauty, but through the Holy Spirit the beauty of the bride of Christ is made manifest. Human effort alone does not avail in our quest for spiritual beautification. The healing of our hearts and the corresponding manifestation of the inner fruits of virtue and beauty can only take place through the power of the Holy Spirit (Gal 5.22–23). That is why the Church continually prays that the Spirit may "come and abide in us." The Eucharist contains an *epiclesis*, an invocation of the Spirit upon the gifts and the community that offers them. In similar fashion all Christian prayer constitutes an *epiclesis*, a cry that the divine *ruach* will *awake* and *come*, and *breathe* upon us. Only when he comes shall *the spices* of our inner beauty *flow* to our Lord and into all the world.

The Man:

5.1I come into my garden, my sister bride;
I gather my myrrh with my balsam.
I eat my honeycomb and my honey;
I drink my wine and my milk.

The Chorus:

Eat, companions!
Drink yourselves drunk on caresses!

The man responds at once, saying that he will indeed *come into his garden* and *gather* its fragrant blossoms of *myrrh* and *balsam*, *eat* his *honeycomb and honey* and *drink* his *wine and milk*. His determination to thoroughly accept her invitation to *eat* such *choice fruits* (4.16) is matched by the totality of his union with her: she is his *sister bride* with whom he feels at one, both soul and body, as close to her as if she were a sister and a spouse. She offers herself completely, and he takes her completely, claiming as his own all she offers to him by repeating the possessive *my* in detailing each of her proffered gifts. He does not tell her that he will take *her* myrrh with *her* balsam, but rather *my* myrrh with *my* balsam. Likewise he says he will "eat *my* honeycomb and *my* honey" and "drink *my* wine and *my* milk." The possessive *my* is repeated eight times in this single verse: the lovers are one.

The lover's dialogue ends with the chorus bestowing a blessing on the lovers, urging them to *eat* and *drink* themselves *drunk on caresses*. The chorus describes the lovers as *companions*, the same word used by the lovers to describe each other (he to her in 1.9, 15, 2.2, 10, 13, 4.1, 5.2, 6.4, and she to him in 5.16). Given that this is a favorite mutual term of endearment, it seems likely that the chorus means to describe the lovers as *companions of each other*, not companions of the chorus. That is, the chorus stands back from the couple, delighting in the mutual companionship and urging them to feast with each other while a discreet dramatic curtain is drawn across the scene.

8

The Woman rejects her lover and then seeks him (5.2–6.3)

The Woman:

₅.₂I was asleep but my heart was awake.
A voice! My beloved was pounding:
"Open to me, my sister, my companion,
my dove, my perfect one!
For my head is drenched with dew,
my locks with the drops of the night."
₃I have taken off my robe;
how can I put it on?
I have washed my feet;
how can I dirty them?
₄My beloved reached his hand through the
    opening,
and my feelings were aroused for him.
₅I rose to open to my beloved;
and my hands dripped myrrh,
and my fingers, liquid myrrh,
on the handles of the bolt.
₆I opened to my beloved,
but my beloved had turned and had gone!
I swooned at his departure.
I searched for him but did not find him;
I called him but he did not answer me.

> ₇The watchmen who make the rounds in the city
>   found me.
> They struck me and wounded me;
> the watchmen of the walls took away my wrap
>   from me.
> ₈I adjure you, O daughters of Jerusalem,
> if you find my beloved,
> as to what you will tell him:
> that I am faint with love.

The various sections of the Song all rehearse and celebrate the varied moods and circumstances of love. In this next section we meet a situation familiar to any couple, that of approach, rejection, regret, and reunion. The lover approaches his beloved with heartbreaking tenderness and yet meets with thoughtless rejection. The beloved regrets rejecting him and seeks to make it up, only to find that she is too late, for her lover has left. She goes after him only to be met with misunderstanding and abuse in the streets. She then adjures the women of Jerusalem not to tell her lover of her adventure, but to say, if asked, that her condition and breathlessness are the result of her being faint with love for him.

The section begins with the woman saying, "I was asleep but my heart was awake." Many commentators have unnecessarily concluded that the woman must be describing a dream.[1] However, there is nothing in the text to support this. Rather, the lines describe the common experience of being in a light sleep: one is truly asleep, but lightly enough that the mind (*heart*, in Hebrew) is attuned to one's surroundings. The inclusion of this state of light sleep is necessary to explain how she is able to hear her lover at the door. Further, there is nothing in the text to indicate that her mind is already filled with thoughts of and desires for him. On the contrary, if she *is* being kept from sound sleep by desires for him, we cannot explain why

[1] Mentioned by G. Lloyd Carr, *The Song of Solomon* (Downers Grove, IL: Inter-Varsity Press, 1984), 130.

she does not leap up to let him in the moment she first hears him knocking.[2]

While in this light sleep, she recognizes *a voice*—that of her *beloved*, who is *pounding* at the door. The lover's noise is no polite and gentle knocking, but a furious hammering at the door (one imagines that his voice is loudly insistent also). The word here rendered *pounding* is the same word used in Genesis 33.13 for the hard driving of flocks, and in Judges 19.22 when the "sons of Belial" are beating at the door, intent upon harming those within. From her bed she hears her lover asking to come in, out of the wet and cold. He implores her by multiplying endearments in an attempt to sway her, calling her "my sister, my companion, my dove, my perfect one."

Such an abundance of sweet talk reveals the intensity of his desire to enter the house. There is no suggestion in the text that he is intent upon sex; his stated purpose is to escape the elements, for his *head* is *drenched with dew* and his *locks* wet *with the drops of the night*. He wants to share her room, not her bed. His message to her is, "Open up and let me come in—it's wet out here and I'm drenched!" The *locks* of the *head* becoming *drenched with dew* would seem natural in the case of someone sleeping outside in Palestine (cf. the abundance of dew in Judges 6.38).

She, however, is reluctant to entertain him at that hour. It is late; she has already retired and gone to bed for the night. She therefore replies, "I have taken off my robe; how can I put it on? I have washed my feet; how can I dirty them?" This reply makes clear that what he is asking for (and she reluctant to provide) is shelter and hospitality, not sex, for if sex were envisioned she would not need to put on her dress, nor dirty her feet.

The man, however, refuses to be put off, and so he *reached his hand through the opening* (literally, "hole"). This refers to the key-hole, for keys were quite large in those days. (In Isaiah 22.22, we find

[2]Making her refusal to admit him only a coy and teasing response to encourage him further does not quite fit either, for teasing will be recognized as such by the one being teased, and this is clearly not the case here. The lover recognizes her words not as a tease but as rejection, which is why he goes away.

reference to a key large enough to be slung over a shoulder.) In other words, the man actually thrusts his hand and arm through the opening in the lock, in a futile attempt to find a way into the house. The sight of him pathetically trying to gain entry causes the woman to have second thoughts—no longer is he is a nuisance but *my beloved*, and her *feelings were aroused for him* (the term *my beloved* is used four times in vv. 5–6, indicating the intensity of her desire). Now she not only wants to give him shelter but sexual comfort as well.[3] That is the significance of saying that her *hands dripped myrrh*, for she apparently took the time to apply myrrh to her bed as a preparation for sharing it with him (cf. the sprinkling of a bed with spices in Prov 7.17).

But in making this preparation she waited too long, and by the time she finally comes to the door and applies her *fingers*, still moist with *liquid myrrh*, to *the handles of the bolt*, he is gone. Her delay in finding and applying myrrh is necessary to the narrative, for if she had flown to the door at once, why is he not still there? Her reaction is extreme—she *swooned at his departure*. The same Hebrew usage (literally, "my soul went out") appears in Genesis 35.18 to describe the death of Rachel, whose soul goes out of her. Here, it is colloquial, as in our own saying, "I could have just died!" When she opens the door to find him gone, she is overcome. She *searched for him but did not find him*; she *called him but he did not answer*. She is not yet combing the streets but looking around and shouting his name, in case he has only gone a few steps and might be recalled. But such was not the case. Her lover is long gone.

She then goes to find him. Many commentators assume, based on a comparison with 3.1–4, that she has no idea where he is, and thus she goes about the city looking for him, even asking help from the daughters of Jerusalem. The text does not say that, however, and it would be unsound to read this meaning into it on the basis of 3.1–4—especially since in 6.1 the daughters of Jerusalem ask her

[3]One might detect a kind of double entendre here, with the hands of the lover at the door seeking an opening and the beloved preparing herself for him.

where he is, on the assumption that she knows the answer. As 6.2 reveals, they are correct. She *does* know: he is at his usual place, in his garden. Some commentators are puzzled by this passage and find themselves reduced to saying, "The logic of this section is strange," and ascribing its lack of logic to "poetic reverie."[4] But there is no lapse of logic here, for the text can be easily read as saying that, while on her way to find him in his garden, *the watchmen who make of the rounds in the city found* her. There is after all no indication that she stops to ask them where he is.

This aspect of the story makes her adventure and injuries all the more poignant, for the watchmen's assault is entirely unprovoked. They had no reason to *strike* and *wound* her or *take away* her *wrap* (a final humiliation and outrage more obvious in that culture than ours). Their motives for this attack are irrelevant and form no part of the narrative. Their actions are portrayed as pure unprovoked thuggery—something sadly not uncommon in any city. They are mentioned here to add pathos to her plight, and to accent the intensity of her desire. Despite such injuries, she continues to seek her beloved. Instead of going home to safety and medical attention, she continues her determined journey to her lover.

Her adjuration to *the daughters of Jerusalem* continues this theme. Like the similar adjurations in 2.7 and 3.5, her words concern a matter of importance. But what is so important? Namely this: *if they would find her beloved*, they must *tell him that* she *was faint with love*. What does this mean? She is not simply lovesick and wanting to find him (although this is clearly true, he will surely find out soon enough without help from the daughters of Jerusalem). Her placing them under oath indicates a matter of greater urgency than a message to her lover that she still loves him. What she insists that the women tell her beloved, if they find him, must have something to do with her negative experience with the watchmen—v. 8 must have some logical connection with v. 7. And indeed it does: what the woman asks of the daughters of Jerusalem is that they convey a false

[4]Thus Longman, *Songs of Songs*, 175.

story to explain her breathlessness and injury. They must not tell him that she is breathless because of what she suffered, but simply that she is *faint with love*. In a nobility of spirit equal to her previous thoughtlessness, she wants to conceal her suffering from the lover, lest news of it cause him to suffer as well. The intended deception of v. 8 is no irrelevant detail, but an essential part of the narrative. Her concern for her lover's feelings cancels out her previous callous selfishness.

In looking at the form of her adjuration, we note that she here omits the words about *the gazelles* and *does of the field*. Her previous adjurations (2.7, 3.5) were occasioned by the woman's desire to let her lover sleep, and spoken in the pastoral idyllic setting of nature (cf. 2.7, where the adjuration is given by the woman from her luxuriant couch in the forest, and 2.16). Here the occasion is different, for the oath is exacted to conceal urban violence rather than to preserve love under the trees, and therefore there is no mention of the forest animals.

Reflection: Rejection and Repentance

This vignette expresses something almost universal in love: the thoughtless rejection of the other through laziness or selfishness, which leads to pain and conflict. Most of the time such conflicts are resolved through repentance and forgiveness. The Song rehearses such a timeless event here and shows the true depth of their love, which can survive and triumph over the occasional thoughtless word or action. In this story the man seeks entry to her home to find shelter from the cold and wet: he pounds on her door, asking to be let in. But she is already dozing in bed—her sleep is still light enough that she can hear him, but she wants to fall soundly asleep. Why should she go to the trouble of bestirring herself and rise up, get dressed, let him in, and entertain him? Let him go away! She has already gone to bed! Despite their love, she is being heartless and selfish.

His pathetic attempts to gain entry finally cause her to have second thoughts, and she regrets her selfish refusal to let him come in. When she finds him gone, she goes out in search of him, making her way to the place where she knows she will likely find him. On her way there, she is assaulted by the watchmen of the city as they make their rounds. Her bruises and scrapes prove the depth of her determination to find her lover.

When this concise drama is transposed into the spiritual setting of the soul's love for the Lord, we recognize in it the story of our own sin and repentance. Our own acts of laziness and selfishness grieve the Holy Spirit and drive God's joyful presence away (Eph 4.30). The woman's delay in coming to the door, even if she is motivated by thoughts of love as she anoints her bed with myrrh, proves disastrous. When she finally comes to the door, she finds him long gone. This tells us that when we are first made aware of our sin we should hasten to repent, without delay. The temptation is always to delay repentance and instead procrastinate, putting off the hour of our humiliation and confession. But if we wish to preserve the Lord's presence in our life, our regret must lead to immediate repentance and the resolve to amend.

The Lord is grieved and his Spirit driven away whenever we sin, but perhaps these verses especially apply to our sins against the poor. In the narrative, the man seeks entry into the woman's house to find shelter against the elements. This fact reminds us of the many in this world who similarly need shelter against the drenching cold of life. The poor, the hungry, the cold, and the lonely we always have with us (Mt 26.11), and these least of the king's brothers have special significance. Our King identifies with these humble ones to the point that he counts our neglect of them as neglect of himself (Mt 25.31–46). When we hear them pounding on our doors late at night, whether with entreaties or in silent need, we must hasten to answer lest the Lord depart from those of us who prefer warm comfort to the sacred demands of hospitality to the world.

The Chorus:

5.9What kind of beloved is your beloved,
O most beautiful of women?
What kind of beloved is your beloved,
that you adjure us like this?

The Woman:

10My beloved is radiant and ruddy,
eminent among ten thousand.
11His head is gold, pure gold;
his locks are fir trees,[5]
black as a raven.
12His eyes are like doves
by streams of water,
bathed in milk,
sitting by pools.
13His cheeks are like beds of spices,
trellises of sweet-scented herbs;
his lips are lilies
pouring liquid myrrh.
14His arms are rounded gold
set with beryl;
his form is carved ivory
wrapped with lapis lazuli.
15His legs are pillars of alabaster
set on pedestals of pure gold;
his appearance is like Lebanon
choice like the cedars.
16His mouth is full of sweetness
and he is wholly desirable.
This is my beloved and this is my companion,
O daughters of Jerusalem.

[5]Hebrew *taltallim*, meaning "uncertain." The Septuagint renders it ἐλάται (*ela-tai*), "fir trees."

In a stylized form of questioning, the chorus of the daughters of Jerusalem responds to her adjuration by asking, "*What kind of beloved is your beloved that you adjure us like this?*" In other words, what is so great about him that he warrants such special treatment? Her love for him is stressed by their calling the man *your beloved* or *beloved* four times in this single verse. The purpose of the question is to provide an opportunity for the woman to describe his beauty and charms at great length, which she does beginning from the top and working her way down.

She begins her glowing description of her beloved as *radiant and ruddy, eminent among ten thousand*—or as we would say, "one in a million." In her description of him as "ruddy," we detect also an element of youthfulness, as when the young shepherd boy David, facing the Philistine Goliath, was described as "but a youth, ruddy, with a handsome appearance" (1 Sam 17.42). His ruddy face has the scrubbed glow of youth. His *head* is *pure gold*—not, presumably a reference to suntan, for he has just been described as being ruddy. Rather, the woman alludes to the dazzling and priceless value of such beautiful features. *His locks are fir trees*, in Hebrew *taltallim*. Although a difficult word to translate, it is probably a reference to his hair being thick and bushy, as well as *black as a raven*.

She spends much time to describing *his eyes*, devoting four lines instead of the usual two she allows for his other features. They are *like doves*, probably a reference to their smoke-grey color, or perhaps their gentleness (as in his description of her eyes in 1.15). The rest of the description has occasioned difficulty among the commentators. The reference to his *eyes* as *doves* by *streams of water, bathed in milk, sitting by pools* may refer to the eye's pupil and iris set in the milky white of the eye, i.e., his eyes are glistening, beautiful, and clear, not bloodshot. His *cheeks are like beds of spices, trellises of sweet-scented herbs*. This passage may refer to his scented beard, with hair growing upon his cheek like *herbs* upon *trellises*. His *lips* are *lilies*, indicating they are fragrant as if *pouring liquid myrrh*. His *arms*[6] are *rods of*

---

[6]Hebrew *yad*, literally "hand," can also mean "forearm," as in Genesis 24.30. Jeremiah 38.12 refers to the armpits as the "armpits of your hands."

gold, set with beryl—possibly a reference to golden armlets set with precious stones. His *form* (his body) is *carved ivory, wrapped with lapis lazuli*; it is white and smooth, draped with expensive clothing. The word here rendered *wrapped* is the same word found in Genesis 38.14, where it describes the act of a woman veiling herself. His *legs* are *pillars of alabaster*, strong and smooth, above *pedestals of pure gold*. We note in this last description that she has described her lover as golden, precious from top to bottom, using the word *gold* for his head, arms, and feet alike. She concludes her glowing praises with the summary that his *appearance* is *like Lebanon, choice like the cedars*—he is tall, majestic, and stately, fragrant and justly famous. She adds to her physical account of her lover a description of his kiss, saying that *his mouth* is *full of sweetness* and he is *wholly desirable*. The visual here gives place to the experiential; all his desirability comes to her with his kiss. After this prolonged paean to her lover, the woman steps back and says one last time to the *daughters of Jerusalem*, "This is my beloved and this is my companion." They asked her in 5.9 to tell them what is so great about him, and why she is determined to shield him from grief and seek him despite her injuries. This is her answer. We can almost see her delivering it with a proud toss of her head.

Reflection: The Beloved Praises Her King

The king praises his beloved for her beauty in 4.1–15, a long section in which he lists her many charms with a wealth of metaphor, working his way down her body. She now does the same, listing his charms with the same multitude of metaphor, and also working her way down. This recitation of the king's private beauty forms the counterweight to the recitation of his public glory found in 3.6–11. Everyone in the city, including the daughters of Zion, got to look upon the king on that day. This sight of the king is for the woman alone.

The woman's praise of her lover's beauty provides us with an image of the Church's experience of the divine beauty of Christ. If

3.6–11 focuses upon the transcendent and exalted glory of Christ seated at the Father's right hand and ruling the world, upholding all things by the word of his power (Heb 1.3), this present passage focuses upon his mercy, tenderness, and kindness. This kind of beauty is manifested in his love for sinners, his acceptance of tax collectors and prostitutes, his refusal to condemn the penitent woman taken in adultery (Lk 5.27f; 7.36f; Jn 8.2f). He deals gently with the broken and bruised of the world, taking care not to quench the smoldering wick (Mt 12.20). He reaches out to the powerless, to the marginalized, to children. Those whom the world despises find welcome with him, and he calls all such weary and heavily burdened souls to find rest (Mt 11.28). Balancing the portrayal of the king in ascended splendor is a portrait of the king in lowliness, girded with a towel and intimately washing the feet of his bride. This is the Christ we encounter in confession, the Physician of our souls and bodies, as we creep to the cross in pain, guilt, and bondage in order to find healing, pardon, and liberation. His beauty beautifies us, and his love makes our woeful hearts sing.

After singing the praises of her king, the woman sums up her fulsome description by saying to the inquiring *daughters of Jerusalem*, who had asked what was so special about him, "*This is my beloved and this is my companion.*" The Hebrew word rendered here as "companion" is *rea*, which connotes a kind of reciprocity between two persons. In Genesis 11.7, it is applied to the workers on the tower. The text states that God confused the workers "so that they cannot understand their neighbor's language." In Genesis 31.49, it describes the reciprocal relationship of Jacob and Laban: they place the watchtower pillar as a border between themselves as a sign that God will watch over between them "when we are hidden each from his neighbor." In 1 Samuel 28.17, it is the word Samuel uses when he tells Saul that God has taken the kingdom from him and given it "to your neighbor, to David." The Septuagint renders the word with the Greek πλησίον (*plēsion*), also used in Mark 12.31 in the commandment to "love thy neighbor." In all these examples we detect a relative equality between a man and his *rea*.

It is all the more remarkable, therefore, that the Church prophetically describes Christ as her beloved: her *rea*, companion, neighbor, friend. This witnesses to the Lord's extreme condescension in emptying himself to take on our mortal nature. Since we bear such frail mortal natures, "He himself likewise partook of the same." In order to save us, "he had to be made like his brethren in all things, that he might become a merciful and faithful high priest" (Heb 2.14, 17)—a neighbor and companion of the people he had made. As a merciful high priest, he reached down tenderly to the most broken, binding up their wounds. It is this beauty, this intimate care, that the woman praises as she remembers her beloved.

The Chorus:

6.1Where has your beloved gone,
O most beautiful of women?
Where has your beloved turned,
that we may seek him with you?

The Woman:

2My beloved has gone down to his garden,
to the beds of spices,
to pasture in the gardens
and to gather lilies.
3I am my beloved's and my beloved is mine,
he who pastures among the lilies.

After such a glowing description, the women of Jerusalem now ask her, "Where has your beloved turned, that we may seek him with you?" Her description impressed them enough that they want to see him for themselves when she finds him. She responds, "My beloved has gone down to his garden, to pasture [his flock] in the gardens and gather lilies." She knew all along where he went after leaving her, for she is on her way to find him. The use of the plural (*to pasture in the gardens*) indicates the richness of his many beds of spices, and so offers an image of his wealth and desirability. The section ends with the woman declaring, "I am my beloved's and my beloved is mine; he who pastures among the lilies." That is, it ends with a declaration of mutual ownership and the woman's devotion to her lover. Having said that he has *gone down to his garden to gather lilies* (6.2), the present reference to him as the one who *pastures among the lilies* (6.3) surely means that the woman will find him there, giving him the love she first intended when he pounded upon her door.

9

The Man praises his beloved's face (6.4–13)

The Man:

₆.₄You are as beautiful as Tirzah, my companion,
as lovely as Jerusalem,
as terrible as an army with banners.
₅Turn your eyes from me,
for they have overwhelmed me.
Your hair is like a flock of goats
descending from Gilead.
₆Your teeth are like a flock of ewes
that have come up from their wash,
all of which bear twins,
and not one among them has lost her young.
₇Your temples are like a slice of a pomegranate
behind your veil.
₈There are sixty queens and eighty concubines,
and maidens without number;
₉but my dove, my perfect one, is unique:
she is her mother's only one;
she is the pure child of the one who bore her.
The daughters saw her and called her blessed,
the queens and the concubines also, and they
     praised her, saying,
₁₀"Who is this that looks down like the dawn,

as fair as the moon,[1]
as pure as the sun,[2]
as terrible as an army with banners?"

While it is possible that this section continues the previous one, so that the lover's praise of his beloved in 6.4f represents what he says to her after they meet in the garden, the loose overall structure of the Song does not encourage such an interpretation. Rather, it seems that here we begin a new section, for certainly the women of 6.1 who were determined to accompany the woman on her journey to the garden are nowhere in sight.

Whatever the connection to the previous poem may be, the lover once again praises his beloved, drawing upon and repeating some of his previous praises. In particular, his praise of her *hair* is drawn from 4.1, her *teeth* from 4.2, and her *cheeks* from 4.3. This repetition may be a simple poetic borrowing of material from one poem to another, but in the context of the total Song it seems that even repeated praises are welcome. Love demands fervency and consistency, not originality. If the repetition is poetically deliberate, it may mean that the beloved delights to hear her lover say it again.

He begins his praise with a striking simile: "You are as beautiful as Tirzah, as lovely as Jerusalem." She may be his familiar friend and *companion*, but despite this there is something about her that inspires awe, occasioning this comparison to two notable cities. Admittedly our own modern cities, with their slums, pollution, overcrowding, and crime, do not position us well to understand the awe that the ancients felt for a city. Cities in the ancient world were much different than our modern ones. First of all they were smaller, and walled. Indeed, a wall was one of the things that defined a city[3] and differentiated it from the surrounding villages. A city was protected by its walls, inside of which life could be lived in all its exciting

[1]Literally, "the white one."

[2]Literally, "the hot one." The same terms for the moon and the sun are found in Isaiah 24.23.

[3]Thus Revelation 21.12: even the heavenly new Jerusalem has walls.

fullness, especially when compared to the sleepy countryside around
it. Looking up at those walls with awe, one saw the city as proud
and regal. Thus Jerusalem is compared to a majestic woman and
referred to as "the daughter of Zion" (Is 1.8; 62.11; Jer 4.31; Mic 4.13;
Zech 9.9), even a "virgin daughter" (2 Kg 19.21). This last reference
is to her status as impregnable and safe from conquest. An ancient
Jew looked upon cities, especially the city of *Jerusalem,* as proud and
majestic. Likewise the city of *Tirzah* in the north, about six miles
from Shechem,[4] was known for its abundant water supply and the
resultant gardens, flowers, and groves. These were not simply *beautiful* and *lovely,* but also *terrible as an army with banners* (literally,
"bannered ones").

If the cities are beautiful and terrible at the same time, the lover
declares that so too is his beloved. Her glance can *overwhelm* him,
causing him to beg that she *turn* her *eyes from* him. We see again
the power of the woman and the power of love: a single glance from
her can reduce him (4.9), and now he repeats this sentiment using
a stirring military image. Her effect is profound. The Hebrew word
ayummah (terrible) used to describe her (*terrible as an army with
banners*) is the same word used to describe the terrifying Chaldean
army in Habakkuk 1.7, while the cognate noun is applied to the teeth
of Leviathan in Job 41.14. Her beauty is so overwhelming that only
the metaphor of a conquering armed host suffices to describe it.
Such beauty is irresistible, and he finds himself quickly and happily
conquered.

After a reference to her *terrible* and almost indescribable eyes,
the man continues to work from the head down, repeating his previous descriptions of her. To this he adds that she surpasses anyone
else at court. Although *there are sixty queens and eighty concubines
and maidens without number,* his beloved is *unique.* The court is

[4]The pairing of Tirzah with Jerusalem may help to date the Song to the time of
Solomon. In the time of Solomon's successor Rehoboam the kingdom was split in
two, with the northern rival king Jereboam making Tirzah his capital (some fifty years
later, King Omri would move the capital to Samaria; 1 Kg 16.23f). It is unlikely that
after the time of Solomon a poet would pair Jerusalem with the hated rival capital.

described in sweeping generalizations, with the *queens* being the wives of the king who can bear heirs to the throne, the *concubines* wives of lesser importance whose children cannot inherit the throne, and the *maidens* the other noble women at court. These numbers are lower than those recorded elsewhere for Solomon (1 Kings 11.3 mentions seven hundred wives and three hundred concubines, though this may well represent hyperbole), but accuracy is not the point. The poet not a statistician, nor accurately recounting the life of Solomon. The lover is not Solomon, but modeled after him; he is every man who has ever been in love. The numbers *sixty* and *eighty* simply mean "many" and provide an opportunity to compare his beloved with many women. She is his dove, his perfect one, and unique. If she considers him to be eminent among ten thousand (5.10), he in turn regards her as incomparable.

No wonder she is described also as her mother's only daughter, the pure child of the one who bore her. The Hebrew word here rendered "pure" is *bara*, meaning "choice, favored." She shines forth as obviously special. The word *bara* is also used in the following verse to describe the sun—like the sun, she is luminous, radiant, shining upon and illumining all who see her. We know she is not literally *her mother's only one*, for the woman makes reference to brothers in 1.6. But she was favored by her mother *as if she had been* her only one, even as God calls Isaac Abraham's "only son," despite the fact that Ishmael was Abraham's son also (Gen 22.2). Such is her glory that she makes her beloved forget about everyone else.

Not only did her biased mother regard her like this, but even the *daughters* at court, i.e., the maidens, *saw her and called her blessed*, along with the *queens* and *concubines*. Everyone who sees her recognized her surpassing excellence, and *praised her* with a kind of awe. It is as if they cannot believe their eyes, asking with wonder, "Who is this that looks down like the dawn, as fair as the moon, as pure as the sun, as terrible as an army with banners?" She is like some kind of celestial phenomenon. One could stand with awe and see *the dawn*, just as the new light of each day looks down upon the

earth and gives joy to everyone. One could see *the moon*, fair in the
night sky, ruling over the slumbering world, or *the sun* above, pure,
blasting, life-giving. Everyone agrees with a kind of amazement that
she is like these: a miracle without explanation, a dominating force
by day and night. For these observers also, the man emphasizes, she
is *as terrible as an army with banners*.

Reflection: The Bride of Christ as an Army with Banners

The dual references to the woman's beauty as "terrible as an army
with banners" has been variously translated. The Hebrew word is
nidgalot. Some[5] understand that its root (*dgl*) means "to look," and
so the phrase means "as terrible or awe-inspiring as these *sights*"
(of Tirzah and Jerusalem). However, the word "terrible" is such a
powerful word (also used to describe the invading Chaldean army
in Habakkuk 1.7) that it is difficult to imagine why Tirzah, with its
natural beauty, large gardens, groves, and abundant water supply,
should inspire such fear. It seems better to understand *dgl* as "to
lift banners," so that the phrase means "bannered ones." The "bannered ones" may refer to Jerusalem and Tirzah when festooned with
military banners, but there is no reason to think that Tirzah had any
real military significance in Solomon's time. "Bannered ones," then,
reads more naturally as a reference to an army. The Septuagint renders it τεταγμέναι (*tetagmenai*, "drawn up in order"), which seems
to reflect the same understanding. This being the case, the man is
describing his beloved twice as *terrible as an army with banners* (6.4,
10). We may interpret this as a reference to the bride of Christ as an
army, the *militia Christi*.

The woman's beauty succeeded in conquering her man; it is the
beauty of Christ's truth in the Church that can conquer and save
the world. The New Testament is filled with an abundance of such
martial imagery. The Church possesses divinely powerful weapons
of warfare, suitable for the destruction of fortresses, and with them

[5]For example Snaith, *Song of Songs*, 88.

she wages war, though not according to the flesh. She besieges every lofty thing raised up against the knowledge of God, and takes every thought captive to the obedience of Christ (2 Cor 10.3–5). We arm ourselves with the armor of God and fight against the rulers and forces of darkness, the spiritual armies of evil in the heavens, wielding the sword of the Spirit, the proclamation to all men of the gospel of God (Eph 6.11–17). In all things we aim to the please the Lord, in whose enlisted service we are, and we continue to fight the good fight (2 Tim 2.4; 4.7). The Church is indeed an army with banners, lifting high the standard of the cross. As we serve the Lord in obedience, as his loving bride, we must serve him also as brave soldiers, for the Church's beauty consists of both her devotion and her bravery.

The Woman:

6.11I went down to the nut grove
to see the blossoms of the valley,
to see if the vine had budded
or the pomegranates had bloomed.
12I did not know myself,
set in the chariots with the prince.[6]

The Chorus:

13Turn, turn, O Shulammite;
turn, turn, that we may gaze at you!

The Man:

Why should you gaze at the Shulammite,
as at the Dance of the Two Companies?

[6]The Hebrew is uncertain, and all translations are tentative. This rendering draws upon that of Pope, *Song of Songs*, 552, 589. The Septuagint also had trouble with the Hebrew and was reduced to transliterating the Hebrew words here rendered "with the prince" as the proper name "Ammi-nadib," despite the apparent meaninglessness of the reference.

After the man's praises conclude, we hear again the voice of the woman. The connection with the previous lines is unclear; she seems not to reply to him immediately, but first begins to reminisce. Verse 12 is among the most difficult of the Song, both in terms of translation and meaning. If we are right about its meaning, it appears that in v. 11 the woman reminisces about her past in order to accentuate the wonderful state of her present. She *went down to the nut grove to see the blossoms of the valley, to see if the vine had budded or the pomegranates had bloomed*—that is, her presence in the countryside was originally just a part of her discovery and enjoyment of spring. She did not know what she was letting herself in for, namely, meeting and falling in love with the king. This interpretation of her actions in valley presupposes the contrast mentioned in v. 12: she contrasts her present joy with the king with her previous prosaic tour of the valley.

The list of the signs of spring—the *nuts*, *blossoms*, *vine*, and *pomegranates*—are not necessarily euphemisms for sex. These do not describe their lovemaking, but rather the background to it. Indeed, such a lush background for their romance only serves to make their love more inevitable. (In the Septuagint reading we find the added phrase, "There I will give you my breasts.") Before she knew what was happening to her, she finds herself swept off her feet: *I did not know myself, set in the chariots with* her *prince*. That is, she can scarcely recognize herself in this wonderful new role, standing beside the king in his royal chariot.

At this point the chorus breaks in, giving voice to the men who are also overcome with her beauty. They bid her to *turn, turn*, that they *may gaze* at her. They are intent on feasting on such beauty. The Hebrew word rendered here as "gaze" is *hazah*, the same word used for the vision that Isaiah "saw" (Is 1.1). Isaiah stared with intensity at the vision that God gave him; the men here want to stare at the woman with the same intensity. The cry of *turn* could mean "turn around" or more likely, "return." If the woman has stepped into the chariot with her lover to depart, this cry could represent their distress at her departure. They cannot get enough of her beauty and so plead with her to stay.

The title with which they address her, *Shulammite*, is otherwise unattested in the Old Testament. Some read it as a corruption of the word Shunammite, i.e., a woman from the town of Shunem. The Vaticanus manuscript of the Septuagint does indeed read "Soumaneitis" (Shunammite), while the Alexandrian manuscript of the Septuagint reads "Soulamitis" (Shulammite), the letter *l* and the letter *n* often being interchanged in Semitic languages. It is possible that Solomon, or someone commissioned by him to compose the Song, remembered Abishag of Shunem, chosen for her beauty to lay in bed to warm an elderly and failing King David (1 Kg 1.3–4), and called the woman of the Song a Shunammite as a kind of literary echo of the famous young beauty. On the other hand, if one retains the Hebrew text's Shulammite, it might be interpreted as a feminization of the name Solomon (*Shlomo* in Hebrew), functioning as a kind of "Mrs. Solomon." Either view is possible, though the first is perhaps preferable.

In response to the insistent demand of the men represented by the chorus, someone replies, "Why should you gaze at the Shulammite [or perhaps, 'at the Shunammite'] as at the Dance of the Two Companies?" This line is problematic also. Since it constitutes a refusal and rebuke of the demand, perhaps it is best interpreted as coming from the king, who shields his beloved from their gaze. That this is the intent of the response is reasonably clear; less clear is what the *Dance of Two Companies* means. The Hebrew word rendered "two companies" is *mahanaim*, the name of the place in Gilead near the Jabbok River where Jacob met a company of God's angels. He called the place "two companies" (or "two military camps") because here his company of men encountered the company of God (Gen 32.1f). We might understand the reference geographically, as in "the dance that they perform in Mahanaim," but this seems unlikely. It is better to take the words to indicate the name of a specific and popular form of dance, one that people liked to watch performed.

Regardless of the precise significance of the term, we understand the main point of the reply: the woman is not to be objectified and gawked at for her beauty, as if she were on display. In the Song her beauty is her gift to her lover, not a commodity to be thrown about casually to anyone who happens to be around.

10

The Man and the Woman spend the night in the open field (7.1–8.4)

The Man:

~7.1~How fair are your feet in sandals,
O noble daughter!
The curves of your hips are like ornaments,
the work of the hands of a craftsman.
~2~Your navel is a rounded bowl
that never lacks mixed wine;
your belly is a heap of wheat
encircled by lilies.
~3~Your two breasts are like two fawns,
twins of a gazelle.
~4~Your neck is like a tower of ivory,
your eyes like the pools in Heshbon
by the gate of Bath-rabbim;
your nose is like the tower of Lebanon,
looking toward Damascus.
~5~Your head is upon you like Carmel,
and the flowing locks of your head are like purple;
a king is captivated by its tresses.
~6~How fair and how delightful you are,
love[1] with delights!
~7~Your stature is like a palm tree,

---

[1]Hebrew *ahaba*, describing love in general (thus 2.4, 5, 7; 3.5; 5.8; 8.6, 7), rather than a pet name for the beloved.

and your breasts are its clusters.
₈I said, "I will climb the palm tree,
I will take hold of its branches."
Oh, may your breasts be like clusters of the vine,
and the fragrance of your breath[2] like apples,
₉and your mouth like the best wine,
going down smoothly for lovers,
flowing over the lips of sleepers.

The man now begins to praise his beloved in her totality. In 6.4–9 he praised her face and countenance, focusing upon her eyes, her hair, her teeth, and her cheeks. Previously, in 4.1–6, he surveyed her from her head down to her breasts; in this final paean of praise he misses nothing. Here he surveys her completely, beginning at her feet and working his delighted way upwards. He delights to look at her, both from the top downwards and from the bottom upwards. From whatever vantage point, she is altogether perfect.

He begins by crying, "How fair are your feet in in sandals, O noble daughter!" Her feet are not the rough and calloused feet of a laborer but dainty and smooth, like those of nobility. He makes special mention of her *sandals*, since sandals were regarded in that day as especially exotic (cf. mention of sandals in Judith 16.9, with its reference to Judith's seductive ploy: "Her sandal ravished his eyes; her beauty captivated his mind").

Working his way upwards, his focus falls upon *the curves of* her *hips*. He pronounces them exquisite, *like* crafted *ornaments, the work of the hands of a craftsman*. There is little point in guessing what kind of ornaments he has in mind: he refers only to the superb craftsmanship and beauty with which she was made.

Verse 2 has occasioned perplexity from commentators. It begins with a description of her *navel*, using the word in Ezekiel 16.4 that denotes the umbilical cord and in Proverbs 3.8, where "navel" represents the core of the body's life, parallel to its bones. The man com-

²Literally, "nose."

pares it with *a rounded bowl that never lacks mixed wine* (Hebrew *mezeg*, a wine to which spices and honey have been added for increased potency). The image, then, is one of a drinking goblet ever full of potent, intoxicating wine. The problem is that although a navel can be called round, like a drinking bowl, it is difficult to see how it could be said to hold wine. Certainly, its small size does not suggest a drinking bowl. For this reason some commentators[3] translate the Hebrew not as *navel* but as "vulva," which is larger and can contain fluid. This rendering has its own problems, however. Apart from the fact that the shape does not seem to fit the image of a round bowl, the indelicacy of the reference does not quite fit the poetic restraint seen throughout the Song. A sense of romantic delicacy demands that such things be alluded to through metaphor, not crassly and anatomically described.[4]

I suggest, then, that the man's reference to the woman's *navel* is a delicate metonymy for all that is found below it. The point of the metaphor is not that a navel physically resembles a round bowl of mixed wine, but that his experience of her *navel* (that is, all that is below it) reminds him of the experience of drinking an ever-flowing inexhaustible *bowl* of intoxicating *wine*. No references to bodily fluids are required. The bowl of wine does not provide a visual image for the navel (or any other part of her body) so much as a metaphor for his enjoyment of it.

A similar degree of interpretive perplexity attends the man's description of her *belly* as *a heap of wheat encircled by lilies*. The Hebrew word here rendered as "belly" is *beten*, used to describe the womb (thus Job 3.11 and Ps 139.13) or the stomach. But how can either resemble *a heap of wheat*? Some have suggested that the image is of a sheaf of wheat tied in the middle; in that case b*eten* should be translated "waist."[5] But the waist is higher up the body than the womb,

[3]For example Longman, *Song of Songs*, 194–95.

[4]For this reason interpretations like Longman's, which regards the "lilies" encircling the woman's "heap of wheat" or belly as a reference to her pubic hair, are to be rejected.

[5]Thus Garrett, *Song of Songs*, 240.

and the Hebrew word rendered as "heap" is not the usual term for a sheaf, but a more general term.

Once again I suggest that the image refers to the man's experience and thus does not imply any visual resemblance. That is, *beten* here means "lap," and the man is describing his experience of lying in her lap, saying that it is as soft as lying upon a heap of wheat. As with the previous discussion of the woman's navel, the point here is not to provide a visual description of her anatomy but an allusion to experience. Just as his experience of lovemaking below her navel is fitly imaged by his drinking from an ever-brimming drinking bowl, so now the experience of resting his head in her soft lap, directly above her womb, is fitly imaged by his experience of lying on a soft heap of wheat in a wheat field. Her belly being *encircled by lilies* refers to their experience of being surrounded by lilies in their forest trysting site: this heap of wheat is not in an open field, but in the lush privacy of their forest. This interpretation is consistent with the other references to lilies in the Song (2.16, 4.5, 6.2–3), where they represent a time and place of private lovemaking.

The man next focuses upon her *breasts*, repeating his praise from 4.5. Moving upward along her body he next praises her *neck*, saying that it is like a *tower of ivory*, a reference to its smooth height and creamy white color. She is not bull-necked, but elegant and graceful. Her *eyes* he praises as *like the pools of Heshbon, by the gate of Bathrabbim*. Heshbon was a city to the east of Jerusalem, home to a large reservoir. Its deep, clear pools full of life-giving water remind him of his beloved's clear and glistening eyes.

His praise of his beloved's nose, which he likens to *the tower of Lebanon looking toward Damascus*, has also occasioned much perplexity among commentators. The phrase can hardly mean that she has a big nose. Some suggest that "Lebanon" means "the cliffs of the Anti-Lebanon mountain range," which are "chalk-colored,"[6] so that "tower of Lebanon" means "the tower which is a white cliff

---

[6]Dianne Bergant, *The Song of Songs* (Collegeville, MN: The Liturgical Press, 2001), 86.

in Lebanon." The mountains of Lebanon do indeed *look toward Damascus*. Certainly we have no knowledge of any ancient structure in Jerusalem called "the tower of Lebanon." If this is so, then the man is praising the whiteness of her nose, a sign of wealth and delicacy in contrast to the sunburnt noses of women who labor in the fields.

He reaches the summit of his praises with the summit of her body: her *head* is like tall Mount *Carmel* in the north of Palestine, majestic and regal, looking down upon the world below. Upon this head he admires her *flowing locks*, which are *like purple*. The word *purple* here describes a shade of deep blue-black (cf. his description of her hair color as black like a flock of goats in 4.1). Even *a king*, he declares, would find himself *captivated by* those flowing *tresses* of unbound hair.

Standing back from her, he cries out, "How fair and how delightful you are!" She is *love with delights!* He has surveyed every part of her, and pronounces her altogether beautiful. As she stands there, her is *stature like a palm tree*, her *breasts* are *like its clusters*. The admiration of visual survey gives place to a determination for tactile caressing. He declares his intention to *climb* that *palm tree* however tall it may be, and to *take hold of its branches*, however out of reach they may seem—that is, the clusters of her *breasts*. In their lovemaking, those *breasts* will taste *like clusters of the vine*, the sweetest wine, and *the fragrance of* her *breath* like sweet *apples* (known as a fruit of luxury). Her *mouth* too, with her kisses, will be *like the best wine, going down smoothly, flowing over the lips of sleepers*.

This last verse has caused endless difficulty for translators and commentators alike. In the first part of v. 9, the man is clearly speaking, yet the latter part of the verse (according to the Hebrew text) describes the wine as "going down smoothly for my beloved [*dodi*]" which is how the woman describes her man, not the man his woman. Accordingly some commentators[7] suggest that the woman here breaks into the man's speech, finishing his sentence for him. This

[7]Garrett, *Song of Songs*, 236; Hess, *Song of Songs* (Grand Rapids, MI: Baker Academic, 2005), 223.

seems unlikely and also would be unprecedented in the Song, where the couple consistently expresses love through dialogue, not interruption. Some therefore suggest emending the Hebrew so as to read "going down smoothly for lovers," which emendation I accept here.

Also troublesome is the phrase *the lips of sleepers*, which commentators have long found problematic given that one cannot drink while asleep. They propose an emendation that would have the wine flowing over "lips and teeth."[8] The result is a fairly colorless image that barely makes sense, for where else could wine go when being swallowed but over lips and teeth? Accordingly I prefer the *lectio difficilior* of the Hebrew text. I suggest that it refers to the happy sleep that overcomes the lovers after their lovemaking, and so the man here says that her kisses will satisfy them like the best wine, sending them to contented sleep.

> *The Woman:*
>
> 7.10I am my beloved's,
> and his desire is for me.
> 11Come, my beloved, let us go out into the field;
> let us spend the night among the henna blossoms.
> 12Let us rise early and go to the vineyards;
> let us see if the vine has budded
> and its blossoms have opened,
> and if the pomegranates have bloomed.
> There I will give you my caresses.
> 13The mandrakes have given forth fragrance;
> and at our doors are all choice fruits,
> both new and old,
> which I have saved up for you, my beloved.
>
> *The Woman*:
>
> 8.1Oh that you were like a brother to me

8The emendation is as old as the Greek Septuagint.

who nursed at my mother's breasts!
If I found you outside, I would kiss you;
no one would disdain me.
₂I would lead you and bring you
into the house of my mother who conceived[9] me;
I would give you spiced wine to drink
from the juice of my pomegranates.
₃His left hand is under my head
and his right hand embraces me.
₄I adjure you, O daughters of Jerusalem,
do not arouse or awaken the love
until he pleases.

The woman responds to his praise by offering her own love afresh, saying, "*I am my beloved's and his desire is for me.*" This differs from her similar declaration of 6.3, when she says, "I am my beloved's and my beloved is mine." Here, her declaration that he belongs to her is replaced by her observation that he desires her. That is, his intense desire for her is the evidence that he belongs to her. She goes to satisfy this desire, inviting her *beloved* to *go out* with her *into the* open *field* and *spend the night among the henna blossoms.* So eager is she for this that she bids him *rise early* with her to *go* out *to the vineyards*, so see how spring has *bloomed* around them. The signs of spring—the *budded vine*, the *opened blossoms*, and the *blooming pomegranates*—mirror their own blossoming love, and will form the background of their night together. *There*, she promises, she *will give* him her *caresses.* She mentions *the mandrakes*, those famous fruits of love (cf. their proverbial qualities as an aphrodisiac mentioned in Genesis 30.14f), along with *all choice fruits* that are found *at* their *doors.* Here we seem to have a picture of the woman looking from her doorway toward the lush spring setting outside, inviting her lover to leave the house and experience the *fragrance* and delights of spring—and of her love, of which these *mandrakes* and *choice fruits*

[9]Thus the Septuagint. The Hebrew reads: "and she/you will teach me."

are images. She emphasizes not merely a few fruits but all *choice fruits, both new and old*. She has a heart full of love to give him, a night full of the varied delights of lovemaking, which she declares she has *saved up* for her *beloved*, including *new* things never yet experienced by him. Her invitation and description of what awaits him outdoors, in the open field among the henna blossoms, is meant to arouse keen anticipation and the impatient ardor of love.

The woman is filled with such affection for him that she regrets that they must leave the city to find privacy in the country, and she laments, "Oh that you were like a brother to me who nursed at my mother's breasts!" Then she would have no reason to refrain from displays of affection; if she *found* him outside where others were, she could *kiss* him and *no one would disdain* her. As it is, societal norms demand that she restrain herself from kissing him when they are in public. Such is her overpowering passion that she finds this difficult to do: if she finds him outside she will not only kiss him, allowing passerby to mistake them for siblings, but also take him firmly to *lead* him and *bring* him *into the house of her mother who conceived* her. By referring to her home as not simply hers but as "the house of my mother who conceived me," she focuses upon their own love-making there—perhaps with the suggestion that she may conceive there. She says that once at the house she will entertain him lavishly, *giving* him *spiced wine to drink from the juice of* her *pomegranates*.

It is unnecessary to transform this image of lavish hospitality into a set of metaphors for her anatomy, making the pomegranate a symbol of her breasts, as some commentators have done.[10] The imagery is more powerful to the imagination if it is barely hinted at: she promises him lavish hospitality, but with an unspoken suggestion that more will be offered than simply *spiced wine*. This suggestion is furthered by the resemblance of the Hebrew word *ashqeka* ("I would give you to drink") with the Hebrew word *eshaqeka* ("I would kiss you") in the previous verse. Note too the subtlety of her offer—she offers him not simply spiced wine from pomegranate

[10]Exum, *Song of Songs*, 248.

juice, but wine from the juice of *her* pomegranates. The use of the possessive "my" hints that she is offering him what is hers, with all this implies. The woman is no ingénue; she knows well that the approach to lovemaking is all about subtlety. The section ends with their lovemaking, with *his left hand under* her *head* and his *right hand embracing* her (as in 2.6), and her customary adjuration to the *daughters of Jerusalem* that they *not arouse or awaken the love* by disturbing him while he sleeps.

Reflection: In the House of the Mother

In this last declaration of love, the woman confesses that she desires the freedom to embrace and kiss her lover publicly, which she could only do if she were his sister and he *a brother* who *nursed at* their *mother's breasts*. As it is, given the cultural mores of their time, such an embrace was only possible if she first *led* him and *brought* him *into the house of* her *mother who conceived* her. There they could find the privacy that their love required, and he would be free to let his *left hand* be *under* her *head* and to *embrace* her with his *right hand*.

This desire finds it fulfillment in the private worship of the Church, and in the division between the Church and the world. Holy baptism separates us from the world, a separation formerly expressed by the solemn and deliberate closing of the doors at the beginning of the liturgy of the faithful. That is, just before the Eucharistic sacrifice is offered, the deacon cries to the doorkeepers, "The doors! The doors!," bidding them guard the doors of the temple against outside and hostile intrusion. This was a necessary security measure during the years when the Church was persecuted by the state. Even after this persecution ceased, the vestigial command to guard the doors still functions to remind the faithful of their separation from the world. When the doors are closed, we find a division between those outside the doors and those inside them, with the unbelievers shut out and the believers shut in. The closed doors thus form a visible and tangible sign that Christians are quite literally the insiders, different from the rest the world. Every time the doors are closed we find ourselves once again in the Upper Room, shut in with our Lord for an intimate act of spiritual communion.

The woman in the Song wants to take her beloved to a place far from prying eyes, for she shares with him something that he gives to no one else but her. It is the same with the Church as the bride of Christ, for in the Eucharist she shares a life, a joy, and a gift of which the world outside knows nothing. When the doors are shut, the bride and her bridegroom quite literally "get a room" together: the Upper Room in Zion, where their spiritual union is consummated and enacted, where she becomes once again "one spirit" with her bridegroom and Lord (1 Cor 6.17). Just as every baptism takes place in the Jordan, so every Eucharist is held in that Upper Room.

This separation of the Church from the world also finds liturgical expression in the kiss of peace. Originally this kiss was exchanged among the faithful, with visitors and catechumens excluded, for they were dismissed before the kiss was exchanged. The reason for their exclusion?—"they shall not give the peace, for their kiss is not yet holy."[11] That is, the catechumens were still outsiders, not yet made holy through baptism and qualified to stand with the holy people of God in the liturgy of the faithful.

These liturgical practices, which have now fallen into abeyance, witness to an abiding truth about the Church, the bride of Christ: she is separate from the world, belonging only to her Lord and his kingdom. Her communion with him therefore takes place in a place of privacy and separation. Although the liturgical event is now open to the public, even televised, this spiritual separation remains, for only those baptized into the Church or received into her bosom may receive the Lord at the chalice. Only they truly stand within the House of the Mother (cf. Song 8.2).

---

[11]From Hippolytus, *Apostolic Tradition* 18. Translation from *On the Apostolic Tradition*, 2nd ed., Popular Patristics Series 54, trans. Alistair Stewart (Yonkers, NY: St Vladimir's Seminary Press, 2015), 124.

11

The Man and the Woman return together from the wilderness (8.5–7)

The Chorus:

8.5Who is this coming up from the wilderness
leaning on her beloved?

The Woman:

Beneath the apple tree I awakened you;
there your mother conceived you,
there she who gave you birth conceived.
6Place me like a seal on your heart,
like a seal on your arm.
for love is as strong as death,
jealousy is as hard as Sheol;
its flashes are flashes of fire,
the flame of Yahweh.
7Many waters cannot quench love,
nor will rivers overwhelm it;
if a man were to give all the riches of his house for
love,
it would be utterly disdained.

This new section, when linked to the previous one, may be read as its culmination. It certainly forms the culmination of the Song as a whole. We remember in 7.11–13 how the woman urges her lover to go with her out into the field, to spend the night in the open country among the henna blossoms. The subsequent lines about her desire to kiss him openly in public and take him from the city streets into the house of her mother does not alter the place of their tryst, which is the countryside, not the city. In other words, her suggestion in 8.2 that they resort to the *house of her mother* must be read as part of her stated desire of what to do if they were confined to the city—not as an indication that they are actually *in* the city. Thus the section ends with the lovers together in the countryside, among the henna blossoms.

Once this is understood, we may correctly understand the significance of the chorus's question, "Who is this coming up from the wilderness leaning on her beloved?" The women of Jerusalem, represented by the chorus, now see the couple returning from their private tryst in the field. Just as in 3.6 Solomon's litter is seen on the horizon, coming into the city from the *wilderness*, i.e., the open country, so now the couple is seen coming up from the same place. They slipped away secretly, but are observed by all upon their return. They see her *leaning on her beloved*, obviously after a night of love. This physical leaning expresses their unity, her dependence upon him, and his committed protection of her. They are one.

The chorus's question of course is rhetorical, serving to focus the reader's attention upon the fact of their togetherness. Accordingly, the question remains unanswered. Instead of replying, the woman speaks to her lover, saying, "*Beneath the apple tree I awakened you.*" The focus remains on their intimate dialogue, made all the more intimate by her leaving the chorus' question unanswered and speaking to her lover alone. She will not be distracted, nor allow her attention to wander away from him.

Her words to him bid him to remember what happened when she woke him up that morning; they are almost a kind of pillow talk, still charged with sexual potency. This is all the clearer when we learn what did happen when she woke him up. The verb *awakened* in 8.5 is the same verb she uses to adjure the women in 8.4: *do not . . . awaken the love until he pleases.* By this adjuration the woman insists that the women of Jerusalem let her lover sleep, because when he awakes his love and passion will awaken with him.[1] Now, by reminding him that she herself *awoke* him, she thereby reminds him of what happened after she did wake him up—namely, more lovemaking. Otherwise, what is the point of her mentioning that she woke him up? This is made clearer by reference of it happening *under the apple tree*, an established image of passion and love, and by the reference to the tree as the place where his own *mother* had *conceived* him.[2] As in 8.2, the reference to conception hints that she too may conceive and bear him a child. Unlike our own day, sexuality in that time was never far removed from the happy thoughts of pregnancy and childbearing. Such conception would have been welcomed by both of the lovers as the fruit and seal of their love.

As the culmination of their lovemaking and unity, the woman asks the man to *place* her *as a seal on* his *heart, like a seal on* his *arm*. Here is the climax of the book, and a summary of its timeless message. Their sexual pleasure, celebrated throughout the book in its many moods, facets, and circumstances by recitations of longing and secret trysts, now finds its fullest expression in exclusive permanent love—in other words, in monogamous marriage. This cry is all the more significant since it is addressed to Solomon—even a literary and not historical Solomon—who was arguably the most famous non-monogamous person in history. Even here, the beloved's heart longs for an exclusive and enduring love. It reveals the essential exclusivity of all true romantic love, and as such deals with a timeless truth, not with the historical Solomon.

She turns to her lover asking that he *place* her *like a seal on* his *heart* and *on his* arm. A *seal* was small engraved cylinder or a stamp that, when pressed upon clay, would leave an impression; it functioned as indication of ownership. By this request the woman

[1] Cf. comments for 2.7 (pp. 49–50).

[2] Note that our reading of 8.2 does not imply that this house is the place where the mother conceived, but simply that it was her *residence* when she conceived. She lived in that house but did not conceive there, but rather conceived under the apple tree.

is asking that she be sealed upon him so that she owns him, and he belongs to her. It is possible that *seal* refers to the cylinder or stamp itself, not to the impression the stamp makes, so that she hereby asks to be his very identity, as close to him as his personal seal. But this understanding creates the problem of how a seal might be worn *on* his *arm*. Cylindrical seals were worn on a necklace cord hanging down one's chest (as in Gen 38.18), or as signet rings (Jer 22.24). There are no similar references to such seals being worn on the arm. Attempts to interpret the seal as a kind of bracelet or to extend the meaning of "arm" to actually mean "hand," so that the seal is signet ring, do not convince.

It seems better to interpret this request as containing an element of symbolism, so that here *seal* does not denote the cylinder itself, but the mark or impression made by it. Such a mark could be made *on* his *heart* itself instead of hanging down *over* it, just above it at chest level. This also allows us to understand the heart in the usual way, as the organ of choosing and volition. The woman is asking to own the organ with which he makes his choices, so that he will never choose anyone other than her. This symbolic understanding of the seal also helps us make sense of the seal being placed *on* his *arm*, for this refers not to *the cylinder* somehow being attached to his arm, but to *the mark* placed on his arm—the arm here representing his strength and his power (cf. the commonly used phrase "the arm of the Lord" in Psalm 98.1; and Isaiah 30.30; 40.10 to denote the Lord's power). By placing her mark of ownership on his arm, she ensures that his strength and vigor will never be given to another woman (another indication that the Song revels in ideal truths, not historical realities).

The reason for such a desire for ownership and fidelity is that *love is as strong as death* and *jealousy as hard* and overpowering[3] *as Sheol*. Death's hold over one is eternal, for none can escape Sheol, the land of dead, after entering it. In the same way love's claim is tenacious,

[3]The Hebrew word *qasheh*, here rendered "hard," contains the idea of conquering; cf. Judg 4.24; 2 Sam 2.17; Is 27.1.

unyielding, eternal. It is jealous, but the word translated here as "jealousy" has none of the unseemly attributes of envy, pettiness, or spite. This *jealousy* is a godly commitment to the beloved, patterned after and resembling the divine jealousy that God has for his people. Yahweh is a jealous God and will allow no idolatrous rivals in our lives (Ex 20.5). He demands our total commitment to him, our exclusive devotion. In the same way, the love that the woman has for her lover also allows for no rivals, but demands complete and exclusive love in return. Its *flashes are flashes of fire*—that is, it manifests itself as a consuming fire, an inferno destroying everything that gets in its way, burning to ashes obstacles, barriers, rivals. It gives all, and demands all. It is like *the flame of Yahweh* itself.

The word translated *flame of Yahweh* is the Hebrew *shalhebetyah*, with the final *yah* read as the divine name Yah, short for Yahweh (as in Ps 68.4). Some prefer to understand the word as a simple superlative such as "an almighty flame,"[4] being nervous about this use of the divine name because of its complete absence elsewhere in the Song, even in the oaths of 2.7, 3.5, 5.8, and 8.4. But its use here at the climax of the Song is appropriate, for the woman concludes her appeal to the man in the strongest terms possible, which include invocation of the divine name. The *flame of Yahweh* is the fire that comes from God himself, the fire that goes before him and burns up his own enemies round about (Ps 97.3). It forms an apt image of the consuming power of the love that can brook no rival. So powerful is this flame of jealous love that *many waters cannot quench it, nor rivers overwhelm it*. The *many waters* here are the vast waters of the sea (the same words are used in Ps 77.19 and 93.4); the *rivers* are not gently flowing rivers, but rushing torrents. Yet even these are powerless to put out love's tenacious fire. Such a love cannot be bought, for *even if a man were to give all the riches of his house for love, it would be utterly disdained*. It is the final part of her appeal to her lover for his exclusive love and his everlasting commitment to her: she offers him a thing more precious than anything else in all the world.

[4]Thus Exum, *Song of Songs*, 243.

Reflection: A Seal Over the Heart

With this section the Song reaches its poetic climax and offers a philosophical reflection on the nature of love. The woman's love is such that it demands absolute exclusivity from her man. This fulfills the repeated declarations of mutual belonging implied in all the imagery and explicitly stated in 2.16 ("My beloved is mine and I am his"), 6.3 ("I am my beloved's and my beloved is mine"), and 7.10 ("I am my beloved's and his desire is for me"). Each completely possesses the other, leaving no room for any rival. This constitutes the true nature of love, first revealed in the primordial declaration that the man and his wife become one flesh, a single organism (Gen 2.24). Neither can bear the thought of sharing the partner with another, whether through the existence of other simultaneous partners, or through the serial polygamy that is divorce and remarriage. The seal over the heart excludes polygamy, adultery, and divorce. Each lover demands complete fidelity from the other and can tolerate no straying, for its *jealousy* is indeed as *hard as Sheol*. This utterance points us toward the ideal that would only come with Christ, far after the days of Solomon and the Old Testament.

When this seal is understood as the close sacramental union of Christ with his bride, we see that true devotion to Christ partakes of this same mutual exclusivity. Christ has no other bride than his church, and we can have no other Lord. Devotion to him therefore excludes any departure from the original apostolic faith. The sexual purity of heart described in the Song finds its spiritual parallel in the purity of the Church's faith and doctrine. Heresy offers us "another Jesus" (2 Cor 11.4), leading us away from simplicity and purity of devotion to Christ (2 Cor 11.3–4). Heresy and false doctrine are not simply erroneous opinions, akin to adding a column of numbers incorrectly and getting the sum wrong. Heresy is matter of the heart, not the head, and thus a form of adultery and idolatry. Indeed, throughout the Old Testament the choosing of false gods, i.e., idolatry, is constantly compared to adultery (e.g., Jer 3.1f; Ezek 16.15f).

If we are true in our love for Christ, we will avoid flirting with a watered-down faith (a form of false doctrine) and frequenting heretical assemblies. The words of Proverbs about the strange woman also apply to the strange doctrines promulgated at such gatherings: "She forgets the covenant of her God, for her house sinks down to death and her tracks lead to the dead. None who go to her return again, nor do they reach the paths of life" (Prov 2.17–19). There is a certain attractiveness to those doctrines that conform more closely to the spirit of the age. Purity of faith in Christ always places us on a collision course with the world, which rewards those who alter the apostolic faith to more closely conform to secular values and opinions.[5] False doctrine thus adorns itself with the bright colors of apparent liberality of mind, tolerance, and enlightenment. If it were otherwise, it would never appear attractive nor ever seduce. In like manner the strange woman utters words that drip honey and are smoother than oil, but at the final judgment these words will prove bitter as wormwood (Prov 5.3–4). Despite the temptation to alter the faith to fit in with the world, we must ever resist such seduction. Adulteration of the faith is indeed a form of adultery. The seal of love upon the heart forbids such betrayal. In baptism we were committed to a form of teaching (Rom 6.17) and betrothed thereby to the Lord, and we cannot depart from that teaching for the sake of more popular doctrines. The seal bids us abide in that first commitment and remain true to our first love (see Rev 2.4). The mutuality of Songs 2.16, "My beloved is mine and I am his" finds its fulfillment in the covenant mutuality of Ezekiel 36.28, "You will be my people, and I will be your God."

---

[5]It is also true that we must avoid the opposite temptation, and defect to join the cold, self-righteous assemblies of schism, which delight in a pursuit of an ever-escalating and elusive purity. Such a house also sinks down to death.

12

The Woman's independence (8.8–12)

The Chorus:

8.8We have a little sister,
and she has no breasts.
What shall we do for our sister
on the day when she is spoken for?
9If she is a wall,
we will build a tier of silver on it;
and if she is a door,
we will panel it with boards of cedar."

The Woman:

10I am a wall, and my breasts are like towers;
so I became in his eyes as one who brings peace.

This section also has occasioned much perplexity, and of the many conflicting interpretations some concern even the identity of the speaker. The plural in vv. 8–9 indicates that these lines come from the chorus, but with whose voice? Who does the chorus represent? Given that it was the responsibility of the men in the family to secure marriage for the womenfolk, it seems best to regard the voices as belonging to men, since the group is discussing what to do with their sexually immature *little sister*. However, there is no reason to suppose, as many have done,[1] that these men are the actual brothers

[1]For example, Longman, *Song of Songs*, 215–16; Carr, *The Song of Solomon*, 171.

of the woman in the Song, already mentioned in passing in 1.6, or that *little sister* with *no breasts* is therefore their term for the woman, past or present. Rather, their plans for what to do with this *little sister* seem intended only to set up a contrast with the woman herself.

The men in vv. 8–9 are considering a *little sister* not yet of marriageable age (hence she has *no breasts*). The controlling image here is that of a fortified city. Hence the mention of a *wall* and a *door*, both of which function to keep people out—an apt image for the concern for the chastity (and thus marriageability) of their sister. There is no reason to suppose that the *door* somehow functions as an image of unchastity, especially since the Hebrew word used here is *delet* (a physical door), not *petach* (a doorway, suggesting greater accessibility, and the same word used in 7.13 to denote an open door). The brothers are not discussing what they will do should their younger sister turn out to be chaste (like a wall) or unchaste (like a door). Doors can be kept closed, after all. This is all the more certain because in both cases the brothers respond to their sister by adorning her—with *silver* (if she is a *wall*) or *cedar* (if she is a *door*). If a girl turned out to be unchaste in that day, it is supremely unlikely that her brothers would speak of adorning her; disgrace and punishment would be the more likely result.

I suggest therefore that the men's deliberations reflect how their society dealt with its young women of marriageable age. If the girl were great and wealthy and desirable, like a vast *wall* of a fortified city, her family would adorn her as richly as a *silver tier* built upon built upon such a wall. If the girl were of lesser nobility, with less wealth and resources (as, for example, a door is smaller and humbler than a wall), her family would adorn her less richly, the same way a *door* might be *paneled with boards of cedar*. In both cases the family does all it can to make the girl more desirable, in hopes of winning a husband. The controlling concern in these verses is the question, "What shall we do for her on the day when she is spoken for?" How can we, the men of the family, secure a good marriage for our sister?

This interpretation (which revolves around the girl's wealth, not her chastity, just as the concern about the woman in 1.6 involves her economic status, not her race) allows us to make sense of the woman's words in v. 10. In contrast to the situation governing marriage, as outlined in vv. 8–9, she boldly affirms, "*I am a wall and my breasts are like towers.*" She is not affirming her virginity, a subject about which there is not a whisper throughout the Song. She is affirming her desirability: she is as *a wall*, i.e., desirable, and her breasts are like its *towers.* The contrast in vv. 8–9 are between more and less desirable girls; she now states that she is desirable not because of her wealth, but because of her beauty. It is because of her beauty that she *became in* her lover's *eyes as one who brings* him *peace* (Hebrew *shalom*) and prosperity. The accent here falls on the phrase "in his eyes." Unlike most girls, she does not need family help to make herself desirable, whether with *silver* or *cedar*. Her beauty alone makes her man desire her. The voice of the family—with all its planning, strategies, and deliberations—is brought forward solely in order to show how she has no need of such things. Indeed, she decisively rejects the family's traditional role. Other girls may need help to find a man, but she does not. The abruptness of her words in 8.10 stands in contrast to all the prior deliberations (nine words, as opposed to their twenty-six) and witness to her independence.

> *The Woman:*
>
> _{8.11}Solomon had a vineyard at Baal-hamon;
> he entrusted the vineyard to caretakers.
> Each would bring a thousand pieces of silver for its
>   fruit.
> ₁₂My very own vineyard is before me;
> the thousand are for you, Solomon,
> and two hundred are for those who take care of its
>   fruit.

Verses 8.11–12 have occasioned at least as much perplexity as vv. 8.8–10. Again, there is disagreement as to who is speaking, a question complicated by whether or not one regards the man in the Song as King Solomon. I regard the man to be a fictive King Solomon, and so assign the lines to the woman.

The woman continues her boast of independence. Verses 8–10 made it clear that she did not need her family's help in getting a man, and now the following verses make clear that she does not need Solomon either, nor is she joining him for his wealth. *Solomon had a vineyard at Baal-hamon* (possibly to be identified with Balamon near Dothan in Judith 8.3), which he *entrusted to caretakers*. Each caretaker farmed the part of the vineyard allotted to him, and would in turn *bring a thousand pieces of silver* to Solomon as payment and rent for the land. The woman, now in full possession of her *own vineyard* (cf. Song 1.6), declares to him that it *is before* her, at her disposal. It belongs to her, not to him. She will give him what he wants (the *thousand pieces of silver* being a metaphor for her love), but she does it willingly. The contrast is between Solomon enjoying the fruits of a vineyard by right of ownership versus enjoying its fruits as a freely given gift. With a dashing flair, the woman adds that she will throw in another *two hundred for those take care of its fruit* and help her with her own vineyard. One should not read into this formula a strict correspondence between her silver and the gift of her sexuality, and conclude that she gives her favors to others as well. The only point here is that she gives her love freely to Solomon: she has more than enough to spare, just as she has more than enough silver to spare.

13

The Man and the Woman's final exchange (8.13–14)

The Man:

8.13O you who dwell in the gardens,
companions are listening for your voice—
let me hear it!

The Woman:

14Flee, my beloved,
and be like a gazelle or a young stag
on the mountains of spices.

Just as the Song began with two verses expressing the longing of
the woman for the king, so it concludes with two verses expressing
her longing once again. The man finds himself separated from his
beloved, who *dwells* in her home amidst *the gardens*. Along with
his *companions*, who have come to know her superlative worth and
are *listening for* her *voice*, he longs to hear her voice and to have her
come among them. He calls out to her, "*Let me hear it!* Come to me
in the city!" She responds that *he* must come to *her*, for she does not
want to join him in the midst of his companions. She wants them to
be alone together, and so bids him come to her in the gardens where
she dwells. Remembering when her *beloved* came to her in times
past, leaping over the mountains and bounding over the hills *like a
gazelle or a young stag* so as to find her behind the windows and the

lattice of her home (2.8–9), she calls out to him again. Let him *flee* his companions, and come to her!

The Hebrew word rendered here as "flee" is *barach*, denoting hurried flight, often from an enemy (thus it is used in Genesis 16.6 to describe Hagar's flight from Sarah, and in Isaiah 48.20 to describe Israel's flight from the Chaldeans). She does not want her beloved to stroll on his way to her but rather make all haste, running to her as fast as he can. Once before he climbed upon the mountains (2.8). Let him come and climb the mountains again—not the mountains separating them, but the mountains of her perfumed breasts, *the mountains of spices*. With this cry of appeal the Song ends—not on a note of satiety, but one of longing. Love can never have enough. It always leaves the lover longing for just one more day.

Reflection: Maranatha!

The Song begins and ends with a note of longing. The woman longs for her absent lover and calls to him, "Flee, my beloved, and be a gazelle or a young stag on the mountains of spices." That is, she calls for him to return, to join her once more for a night of love.

It is significant that both the Song and the book of Revelation end in the same way—with the bride calling her bridegroom to come to her. In the latter love song, the bride calls, "Come, Lord Jesus!" (Rev 22.20). Here, she calls out for him to *flee*, with all the speed of *a gazelle or a young stag*. The night upon *the mountains of spices* witnesses to the unending joy of the age to come, when the bride will forever enjoy the things that God has prepared for those who love him, things which eye has not seen and ear has not heard, and which have never yet entered into the heart of man (1 Cor 2.9).

It is significant, too, that the Song ends on a note of longing rather than one of satisfaction. It is not the case that the love of this bridegroom will grow old, or that the bride can ever reach satiety. Human love may grow stale with age, but not so the love of the bridegroom. This love can never produce satiety but leads always into newer and greater joys, things previously undiscovered and unimagined. St Paul in Ephesians 2.7 speaks of God showing us the surpassing riches of his grace in the *ages* to come (note the plural). In the endless ages to come we will never reach fullness or see the end of our growth in joy. We might imagine that eternal life could become boring at some point, that we might reach a plateau from which no further growth in joy is possible. As St Gregory of Nyssa intuited with his doctrine of *epektasis*, or eternal growth in joy and in God, it will not be so. The longing note on which the Song ends prophesies of our soul's endless longing, which will find continual and eternal gratification. God is infinite, and there will always be more of him for us to discover. No wonder then that the woman calls to her *beloved* to *flee* his companions and hurry to her. She can hardly contain herself or wait for their joy to begin again. In the woman's voice of longing we hear our own voice calling to the Lord, "Let grace come and let the world pass away.... Maranatha."[1] We have had enough of the world and its fleeting, fading joy. We desire to be with our bridegroom, united in a joy that will never end.

Conclusion: Listening to the Lyrics

We began this volume by noting that we live in an age of confusion over many things, including gender and sexuality. In this age of disorder, muddle, lies, and perplexity, the clarity that the Song of Songs offers us is all the more important. It offers us truths about things above and things below, about the nature of God, the nature of human beings, and how humanity is meant to relate to God. When read in the allegorical transposition we have suggested, the Song has many things to teach us about God. Now more than ever, we need to listen to its lyrics.

---

[1] From the *Didache* 10.6. Translation from *On the Two Ways: Life or Death, Light or Darkness: Foundational Texts in the Tradition*, Popular Patristics Series 41, trans. Alistair Stewart(-Sykes) (Yonkers, NY: St Vladimir's Seminary Press, 2011), 40.

First of all, it reveals God as Lover, that is, as masculine, with all that this typology implies.[2] He is King, not queen; Seeker and Wooer, not sought and wooed; the active, not passive; the Giver and not the receiver; Life-giving Father, not life-bearing mother. That is, he is God, not a goddess. Scripture offers us these truths about him even though the divine nature is beyond gender and anatomical sexuality. Scripture consistently presents the deity of Israel and of the Church as masculine, in the sense that Yahweh had no eternal consort: he is purely masculine, for he eternally begets the Son without a mother. There is nothing feminine, passive, or derivative about the Holy Trinity; modern attempts to remake God into a goddess, or to portray him in strictly gender-neutral terms, are to be resisted. It is true, of course, that female similes for God are used in the Scriptures (not surprisingly, since God as creator of both genders knows both the male and the female "from the inside"). Thus Isaiah 66.13 speaks of God as being like a comforting mother, and Christ in Matthew 23.37 says he wants to gather Jerusalem the way a hen gathers her brood of chicks. But these similes are never confused with the authoritative metaphors or names of God, or allowed to overthrow the priority of the normative masculine imagery that consistently undergirds the Church's liturgy. The church confesses God as King, never as queen, and the references in Isaiah about God's maternal care (or his crying out like a woman in labor in 42.14) have never been allowed to supplant the authoritative names by which God is known.

Despite its current cultural unpopularity, this truth about the masculinity of God is essential to our relationship with him, for it tells us that he is the One who seeks us, the Mighty One who wages war on our behalf against Satan, sin, and death. Despite occasional talk about "humanity's search for God," humanity, taken as a whole, is not searching for God. Nor does humanity need to undertake such a search, for God is not lost. Humanity is lost, and manifests its plight by running from God and by choosing idols, whether they

---

[2]I am indebted to Dr Edith Humphrey not only for help throughout this work, but especially for insights in this paragraph.

are constructed out of physical stone or abstract ideology. Mankind is the lost sheep that has gone astray, the idolater that has exchanged the glory of the incorruptible God for an image in the form of corruptible things (Rom 1.23), the girl who betrayed her savior and benefactor by spurning his loving care and turning to other lovers (Ezek 16.15f). Yet despite humanity's rejection of God, he continually searches for the lost, illumining consciences, sowing ideals in every heart and religion. He calls Abraham, creates Israel, and finally comes to live among us as the incarnate Word.

In all this searching, the Lord proves himself to be lover, the active giver, the wooer, and we find our salvation and fulfilled human destiny in allowing ourselves to be found by him. Ours is the subordinate role of beloved, the passive receiver, the wooed. Pseudo-theology and New Age spirituality may choose to present salvation as self-realization, as a task of liberating hidden potential to find our inner divinity. This conception is a lie. What do we have that we did not receive? (1 Cor 4.7). We are saved by grace, and there is nothing that we possess which is not God's free gift. Apart from him, we can do nothing; all peace comes from above. Here is the typological image of the bride of the Song, the one who is sought out and enriched by her king. The mutuality of their love does not imply their essential equality. He is the king: she only becomes royal because he makes her so. The Song teaches us our true place in the cosmos—that of loving nuptial submission to our Lord and King.

Second, the Song also reveals the characteristics of our human nature as a binary phenomenon. As our relationship with God is a binary one, with Christ the masculine bridegroom and humanity called to be his feminine bride, so our sexual relationships with each other are binary as well. The first and most obvious fact about the Song is that it is a sexual song about a man and a woman, and this fact is fundamental. All authentic sexuality is binary, expressed between man and woman, and exclusive as well, as the couple's repeated declarations of devotion prove (even apart from the actual circumstances surrounding the historical Solomon). In this binary sexuality there can be no room for polygamy or polyandry. Hetero-sexual monogamy is celebrated as the pattern for all. Today such traditions in western culture are under assault, and the very concept of fixed gender is being challenged. One now has an array of choices, an ideological menu of sexual options including homosexuality, bisexuality, and transgenderism. Some assert that gender is fluid, even self-created, an entirely subjective choice that one makes with no relationship to chromosomes, anatomy, or hormones. Being born with an exclusively female anatomy and set of hormones, we are told, need not make one a girl. Physicality need not dictate gender.

For Christians, human sexuality is freighted with transcendent significance, for it reflects the love between Christ and his bride the church. Animal sexuality, of course, is not freighted with any such significance, hence any "homosexual" activity found in the animal kingdom is irrelevant to a Christian understanding of human sexu-ality. For Christians, human sexuality draws its binary nature from its calling to reflect the binary relationship of Christ and his Church. Just as the Church is feminine to him (his bride, not his husband), so must the partner of a man be a woman. To alter this divine con-figuration, which according to St Paul was prefigured and revealed in the Genesis creation stories, in order to allow marriage between two men or two women[3] is to deny that human marriage can carry any such semiotic significance at all. Human sexuality, no longer different in essence from animal sexuality, becomes mere "mating," although of course a mating that may be accompanied by emotional commitment and perhaps sentiment. Our secular culture, which accepts and celebrates homosexual unions as true marriage, also recognizes as normal such indiscriminate mating, usually called "hooking up." Such a linkage is to be expected, for secular culture has already stripped sexuality of any transcendent significance.

The Song of Songs calls us back from the abyss of such madness to sexual sanity through its concentration on the interplay between

[3]Or perhaps three or more partners, for if there is no divine pattern for marriage, why should it be confined to two people?

one man and one woman, with a relentless emphasis on the physical. The very physicality of their relations proved too much for many in the ancient world, especially those raised with a keen appreciation of Greek philosophy. St Gregory of Nyssa, for example, felt compelled to begin his first homily on the Song with a lengthy disclaimer, insisting that, all appearances to the contrary, the Song is not ultimately about sex:

> You who in accordance with the counsel of Paul have "taken off" the old man with its deeds and lusts like a filthy garment (Col 3:9) and have clothed yourselves by purity of life in the lightsome raiment of the Lord . . . hear the mysteries of the Song of Songs. Enter the inviolate bridal chamber dressed in the white robes of pure and undefiled thoughts. If any bear a passionate and carnal habit of mind . . . let such persons not be imprisoned by their own thoughts and drag the undefiled words of the Bridegroom and Bride down to the level of brutish, irrational passions; let them not because of these passions be constrained by indecent imaginings.[4]

Here Gregory seems to fear that his hearers will take his words in a lascivious spirit, welcoming the imagery of the Song for their titillating or pornographic value. (Perhaps this is what Rabbi Akiba feared when he famously said, "He who sings the Song of Songs in wine taverns as if it were a vulgar song forfeits his share in the age to come."[5])

But there is a third way as well, midway between the allegory and the wine tavern: the way of godly erotic love. One suspects that some philosophizing Christian writers of old surely regarded godly erotic love as a contradiction in terms, but I suggest otherwise. Perhaps those whose unworthy reception of the Song was feared by St Gregory and Rabbi Akiba (were there really that many?) welcomed

[4]Gregory of Nyssa, *Homily* 1 (*GNO* 6:14–15). Translation in *Homilies*, 15.

[5]Quoted in William E. Phipps, "The Plight of the Song of Songs," *Journal of the American Academy of Religion* 42.1 (1974): 82–100, at 85.

the mention of breasts and legs for their titillating value. But anyone who is truly in love with another person, as the man and the woman in the Song are in love with each other, will not focus on mere anatomy. The king in the Song does not want any breast, but only the one belonging to his beloved. The woman in the Song does not want just any caresses, only those coming from her king. The physical members are valued because they belong to the other, becoming the pathway to deeper union with that other.

In the end all the references to anatomy in the Song testify to the importance of physical features—whether they be breasts, legs, or chromosomes—in determining sexual roles and gender identity. The higher cannot stand without the lower, just as a tall tree grows only if it is rooted deeply in soil. High and holy things such as gender identity, sexual roles, romantic love, and mutual self-giving only exist and thrive when rooted in the soil of the physical. If mere anatomy is lower on the scale of being than mutuality and self-sacrifice, it forms the foundation of being nonetheless. As St Paul reminded us, "The spiritual is not first, but the physical"[6] (1 Cor 15.46). Few things are more physical, set, obvious, and lasting than anatomy. Rarities notwithstanding, anatomy is constitutive for gender.

The final word must be about love. We have insisted in this volume that the Song of Songs is not just about sex but about love, both divine and human. The latter obviously includes sex, but is not confined to it. The love that is the subject of the Song encompasses divine love also, which is why the insights of human love may be transposed so as to gain insights about divine love as well. Here there is distinction without division, for love is one.

Before the world came to be, there was love: the inter-personal love between the persons of the Trinity. When the world was created out of love, the Lord poured that love out upon all his works. He created the world as binary, so that in the combination of the two genders there might be life and the world would continue to exist. Humanity was created to reflect God's love in a special way, using

[6]"Physical" translates ψυχικός, a notoriously hard word to translate.

its binary gender not only to reproduce and continue the race, but also to reveal the higher possibilities of mutual love. Gender differences are essential, for they allow for a complementary mutuality, each enriching the other with a gift that only the other gender can give. Binary sexuality is called to carry these higher purposes, which some call romance, but married couples recognize as so much more. The erotic attraction each feels for the other calls the couple to self-sacrifice, bidding the wife to surrender to the husband, and the husband to lay down his life for the wife (Eph 5.22 f). In a world that values sex for the gratification and pleasure one can *receive*, a Christian approach to sex inverts such selfishness and values sex for the pleasure it can *give*. That is why St Paul tells husband and wife that neither has authority over their own bodies, but rather each has authority over the body of the other (1 Cor 7.4). In its inversion of worldly sexuality, married sexuality becomes the arena for mutual service, wherein the partners are concerned not with their own needs but with meeting the need of the other. Eroticism in this mutual love becomes the path to self-transcendence, leading one to the doorsteps of holiness and the kingdom of God, for such eroticism is not about sex, but rather self-denying love. Having learned the path of mutual service, the lovers can offer their love to their heavenly Lord also, together submitting to him as part of the spotless bride of Christ.

Thus loves suffuses everything, because God is love. Mere binary sexuality becomes mutual service and love, and this in turn becomes the Church's love for her Lord. The Song of Songs is not just about the sexual love between one man and one woman, or even about the sexual love between men and women in general. It is also about God's love for us, and our saving return of that love to him. This love may begin in this world, but it will survive it. When the sun has burned itself out and all the stars have gone cold and all the galaxies have run down, this love will still live, and thrive, and grow. At the end of the age, the bridegroom and his bride will still find mutual delight. Even now we can hear his approaching footsteps as we lift up our hearts to the final bridal chamber, clothing ourselves in the fine linen of righteousness. Come, Lord Jesus! Hurry, and be a gazelle or a young stag upon the mountains of spices.

Works Consulted

Bergant, Dianne. *The Song of Songs*. Collegeville, MN: The Liturgical Press, 2001.

Carr, G. Lloyd. *The Song of Solomon*. Tyndale Old Testament Commentaries. Downers Grove, IL: InterVarsity Press, 1984.

Duguid, Iain M. *The Song of Songs: An Introduction and a Commentary*. Downers Grove, IL: IVP Academic, 2015.

Exum, J. Cheryl. *Song of Songs, A Commentary*. Louisville, KY: Westminster John Knox Press, 2005.

Garrett, Duane. *Song of Songs*. Word Biblical Commentary, vol. 23B. Nashville, TN: Thomas Nelson, 2004.

Gledhill, Tom. *The Message of the Song of Songs*. Downers Grove, IL: InterVarsity Press, 1994.

Gordis, Robert. *The Song of Songs and Lamentations*. New York: KTAV Publishing House, 1974.

Gregory of Nyssa. *Gregory of Nyssa: Homilies on the Song of Songs*. Translated and edited by Richard A. Norris Jr.. Atlanta, GA: Society of Biblical Literature, 2012.

Hess, Richard. *Song of Songs*. Grand Rapids, MI: Baker Academic, 2005.

Longman III, Tremper. *Song of Songs*. New International Commentary on the Old Testament. Grand Rapids, MI: Wm. B. Eerdmans Publishing Co., 2001.

Murphy, Roland E. *The Song of Songs*. Minneapolis, MI: Fortress Press, 1990.

Norris Jr., Richard A., trans. and ed. *The Song of Songs: Interpreted by Early Christian and Medieval Commentators*. Grand Rapids, MI: Wm. B. Eerdmans Publishing Company, 2003.

Pope, Marvin H. *Song of Songs: A New Translation with Introduction and Commentary*. Anchor Bible series. Garden City, NY: Doubleday & Company, 1977.

Snaith, George B. *The Song of Songs*. Grand Rapids, MI: Wm. B. Eerdmans
    Publishing Company, 1993.